Inclusive Practice for Learning Support Assistants

Inclusive Practice for Learning Support Assistants explores the role of the LSA and, drawing from first-hand interviews, sheds light on a variety of LSA experiences and perspectives, detailing the (often hidden) aspects of their work to support the learning of SEND and neurodivergent students. Covering key areas including wellbeing support, challenging behaviour and student independence, chapters:

- Provide LSAs with practical tips and reflective insights to improve their work supporting children and young people in schools
- Explore dialogic education and assistive technologies, with much-needed reflection opportunities
- Include guidance on working with students one to one as well as in small groups
- Offer advice on how LSAs and teachers can foster strong working relationships in class.

This informative and accessible guide will give both new starter and more experienced LSAs a strong and holistic understanding of the role, inclusive practice and where they can really make a difference for their students. It will be valuable reading for LSAs, as well as the teachers and SENCOs who work closely with them.

Zoe Hosier currently works as a learning support assistant in the sixth form college sector, where she runs group study skills workshops and supports SEND students to access their learning. She studied education at Homerton College, and her research interests currently include grounded practitioner knowledge and the LSA contribution to educational inclusion.

"This book, written by LSAs for LSAs, is a new must-read. Zoe acknowledges that the role of the LSA is often poorly understood but uses each chapter to unpack and unpick that role and empower both new and experienced LSAs to be their most effective and reflective. The book explores key cornerstones of practice for LSAs including fundamental but often overlooked aspects of developing positive relationships with colleagues and students. It acknowledges and discusses the sometimes overwhelming early days in role when LSAs are flooded with training and information, and provides top tips and anecdotes on how to manage this proactively. The book is written with clarity, does not shy away from trickier areas of inclusive practice, and is a must-read for anyone working in a primary or secondary classroom."

Lucy Bullen-Smith, *SENDCo, University of Cambridge Primary School*

Inclusive Practice for Learning Support Assistants

Practical Tips and Reflections from the LSA Perspective

Zoe Hosier

LONDON AND NEW YORK

Designed cover image: Getty Images

First published 2026
by Routledge
4 Park Square, Milton Park, Abingdon, Oxon OX14 4RN

and by Routledge
605 Third Avenue, New York, NY 10158

Routledge is an imprint of the Taylor & Francis Group, an informa business

© 2026 Zoe Hosier

The right of Zoe Hosier to be identified as author of this work has been asserted in accordance with sections 77 and 78 of the Copyright, Designs and Patents Act 1988.

All rights reserved. No part of this book may be reprinted or reproduced or utilised in any form or by any electronic, mechanical, or other means, now known or hereafter invented, including photocopying and recording, or in any information storage or retrieval system, without permission in writing from the publishers.

Trademark notice: Product or corporate names may be trademarks or registered trademarks, and are used only for identification and explanation without intent to infringe.

British Library Cataloguing-in-Publication Data
A catalogue record for this book is available from the British Library

ISBN: 9781032769684 (hbk)
ISBN: 9781032769677 (pbk)
ISBN: 9781003480648 (ebk)

DOI: 10.4324/9781003480648

Typeset in Optima
by Deanta Global Publishing Services, Chennai, India

Data availability statement:
Participants consented for their anonymised data to be published in this book, and to be shared solely with the author's publishing team upon request. Consent was not given for their data to be shared in any other manner, so supporting data is not available.

Contents

	Acknowledgements	vi
	Introduction	1
1	**Defining the LSA: what the LSA is (and isn't)**	11
2	**The LSA and wellbeing support**	34
3	**Strong teacher–LSA working patterns**	60
4	**Responding to challenging behaviour as an LSA**	83
5	**Knowing when to take a step back: supporting student independence as an LSA**	108
6	**The dialogic LSA**	136
7	**Assistive technologies for LSAs**	152
8	**Looking to the future: redefining the LSA?**	174
	Conclusion	191
	Index	195

Acknowledgements

I would like to thank my mum and my sister, for their love and support. Thank you also to JD, for never failing to make me laugh. I send my thanks to my teachers from Down High and my lecturers from Homerton College, who have inspired me to keep thinking and writing about education. I greatly appreciate everyone who took the time to read my chapter drafts and to provide feedback, and I would like to thank my editor Clare for her guidance and encouragement. I am grateful to everyone in the Additional Learning Support Department for their help with this work: I am lucky to work with such supportive and kind colleagues. This book is dedicated to LSAs, and all those working in SEND support.

Introduction

I often think back to when I was set to embark on my work as an LSA for the first time. I had Googled the LSA role to find out more about it, and I remember being struck by the limited number of resources that had been written by LSAs. Reading a book such as this – one that had been written by LSAs for LSAs – would have helped me to fully understand what I was about to take on. I feel it would have aided my practice and made things easier for me during the transitional period when I was settling into my role in the sixth form college sector. I have now, with the support of many brilliant people, had the opportunity to write the book that I wish had been available to me when I began my own journey as an LSA. I hope it will be useful to others in the field who are interested in inclusive education and refining their student support practices.

One of my key motivations in writing this book has been to elevate the **LSA perspective** as it relates to inclusive education. LSAs are the boots on the ground when it comes to SEND support in schools – the sole purpose of their work is to support the educational outcomes of students with additional learning requirements – yet the role has remained largely under-examined within the literature (McConkey & Abbott, 2011). Moreover, the work of LSAs has been scrutinised within the field (Gray et al., 2007; Muijs & Reynolds, 2003; Webster & Blatchford, 2015), particularly when it comes to concerns around pupil over-reliance and LSAs acting as a barrier to the learning of SEND students (EEF, 2021). I have sought over the course of this work to actively engage with some of these concerns, whilst providing some reflective tips that LSAs may use to boost student independence and encourage direct interaction between students and teachers. There remains a need, however, for the voices of LSAs to be heard, given their work in support of students with SEND, and my goal in writing this book has been to craft an intentional space that explores their insights, experiences and grounded knowledge.

I have designed this book with a **holistic** view of the work of LSAs in mind. The LSA role can be quite poorly understood and under-appreciated within education (Farrell et al., 1999; Hall & Webster, 2023; O'Brien & Garner, 2001), and I have noticed a tendency for LSAs to be viewed as prompters, note-takers or general support workers. Although these are indeed aspects of the role, it is collectively much broader than that. LSAs draw on a range of skills to support their students each day. The role is multifaceted as LSAs are often required to provide emotional support to students, build strong relationships with teaching colleagues and respond effectively to behaviour that is often complex and highly challenging. LSAs must support their students to be independent, judging when is best to 'take a step back' in the interests of fostering student agency. Many LSAs also use specific dialogic questioning strategies, and a range of assistive technologies, to enable their students to access their learning in an optimal and engaging manner. The tapestry of being an LSA is rich, and I have found these to be some of the key threads. This book thus examines each of these areas in detail. Each chapter features practical tips and reflective questions, inviting readers to consider these areas of their practice and their application to their current working patterns and contexts.

It is important to acknowledge from the outset that this work is **qualitative** in nature. This means that it is underpinned by personal views, insights and anecdotes. Its findings cannot be generalised, as my aim is to centre LSA perspectives and to examine their views on supporting students across a range of specific areas that I explore in Chapters 1–8. My own reflections, which have been woven into this book, have also largely been shaped by my own experience as an LSA, as I currently work in a sixth form college in an affluent area in the east of England. My degree in education, which I gained in 2022, has also shaped many aspects of this work, particularly my theoretical focus on dialogue in Chapter 6 and my exploration of mediative and restorative approaches to challenging behaviour in Chapter 4. My undergraduate studies have had a strong influence on this work, as I had the opportunity to attend lectures given by Professor Rupert Wegerif, who founded a seminal theory of dialogic education in Cambridge, and Professor Hilary Cremin, whose work has had a strong impact on the study of conflict resolution in schools. This book has, moreover, been born out of collaboration: it features direct quotes, insights and reflections from LSA interviewees. It simply would not have been written without their participation, and I am very grateful for their time, enthusiasm and support.

This work is the product of my own personal reflections as an LSA, and it has also been informed by a diverse set of **interview data** that I collected over the course of 2024. Thirty-one people with SEND support backgrounds have contributed to this book via interview: I interviewed 17 LSAs, five of whom were colleagues that I already knew and was familiar with. I additionally interviewed a learning coach, a teaching assistant, a teaching support assistant and a higher-level teaching assistant, and I facilitated a research-based interview workshop with seven TSAs to discuss their student support practices. I was also keen to speak with LSAs who had left the profession and, to this end, I interviewed two former colleagues who no longer worked as LSAs, in addition to one former learning support mentor (LSM). The interviewees I spoke to worked in a range of educational contexts that included sixth form and further education (FE) colleges, as well as primary, secondary, grammar, private and international schools.

The interviews were semi-structured in nature: I sent the interviewees a list of questions in advance, leaving ample follow-up space for them to express their thoughts during our discussion. Our interviews were recorded using Teams software, and I utilised the Teams transcription function to generate a full interview transcript for analysis. I encountered some initial barriers when reaching out to participants for the book: LSAs lead incredibly busy working lives in schools, and many simply did not have enough time to participate in book interviews with me. Over time, I therefore developed a more flexible approach to data collection by giving participants the option to contribute their views and ideas via email (one LSA opted to do so). In addition to the interviews I carried out with LSAs, I also interviewed four of my teaching colleagues as I was keen for their perspectives to be included in Chapter 3 of the book, which examines teacher–LSA working dynamics. Two of them opted to contribute via email, and I met with the other two teaching participants outside of class to discuss their views on optimal working patterns with LSAs.

The interviews I conducted were incredibly interesting and insightful: many of the LSAs I spoke to were very passionate about their work with students. I updated my list of interview questions over time as the themes of this work evolved, and I purposely asked open-ended questions in the interest of allowing dialogue and reflection to flow more freely. Although the interviews were rich when it came to the personal insights of LSAs and teachers, my sample would undoubtedly have benefited from further diversity, particularly in terms of size, educational setting and regional variation. Every stage of my research process was informed by **ethical** guidelines from the British

Educational Research Association (BERA). Participants were provided with a consent form that clearly stated the intention of the book, and I informed them that they could withdraw from the interview at any time should they wish to do so. I actively welcomed LSA feedback on the manuscript throughout the writing process, as I was keen for participants to voice their views on the work prior to its publication. I have also been intentional about the use of quotations throughout this book: quotes have, with the exception of some very minor edits for clarity, been included verbatim to ensure that the voices of LSAs are actively and organically heard.

Chapter 1 engages with **what it truly means to be an LSA**. The LSA is widely conceptualised as an academic assistant who supports students with SEND to fully access their learning (Fox, 2003). This chapter focuses on lesser-known aspects of the LSA role, however, with a specific focus on the hidden work of LSAs that can often go unnoticed in education. I examine the work of LSAs in support of inclusive education, and I embrace a holistic conceptualisation of the role, focusing on its unique challenges and some of the misconceptions surrounding it. I consider some intrinsically pastoral elements of the work of LSAs in this chapter, examining themes such as LSA ethics of care and the centrality of relationship building to the work of LSAs – 'the work (of the LSA) is iterative – in other words, it is hard to generalise. Each student is different and needs to be "read" individually as you go along. What works for one may not work for another.' I also examine some of the factors that can shape LSA working crafts, as every LSA moulds their practice based on individual factors such as their educational background, school context and knowledge of their students. I reflect on the terrain of navigating 'neurotypical' expectations as an LSA in this chapter, and I discuss my own LSA working craft which has been shaped strongly by my undergraduate degree in education and my interest in dialogue. The voices of LSAs also hold a central position within this chapter. I highlight individual LSA definitions of the role, weaving in direct quotations which explore what their work means to them on a personal level.

Chapter 2 considers the pastoral work of LSAs. I highlight the centrality of **wellbeing** support to the work of LSAs, particularly in light of ongoing post-Covid wellbeing issues that continue to shape the lives of young people (Wright et al., 2021; Prince's Trust, 2022). I explore the specific LSA vantage point as it relates to safeguarding, and I provide numerous strategies that LSAs can use to support student wellbeing in education, from active listening to little chats and small check-ins. I consider the role of the LSA as a motivator in this chapter, providing tips and reflections that LSAs can use to support pupil self-esteem and confidence in their academic abilities. This chapter additionally examines the importance of professional signposting and not 'overstepping the line' when it comes to supporting student wellbeing as an LSA. I conclude with a discussion around LSA wellbeing given the demands and challenges of the role, and I provide tips and reflections to help LSAs reduce the risk of emotional burnout over the course of their work.

Chapter 3 examines the working relationship between LSAs and **teachers**, as the strength of this relationship is integral to the academic outcomes of SEND students (ETF, 2019). I provide tips for both LSAs and teachers in this chapter, highlighting the importance of introductions and getting to know individual working patterns. I encourage LSAs to establish themselves as a supportive classroom presence for teachers, and I prompt teachers to consider how they may optimally work with LSAs in class, whilst benefiting from their knowledge of students and SEND to the fullest extent. I provide insights into what to avoid when working together, and I emphasise the importance of working in partnership as a team ('it should be very close collaborative work'). I consider communication strategies such as class check-ins and corridor chats, as it is important for LSAs and teachers to have effective systems of communication to exchange key information and pupil progress updates. This chapter also emphasises the importance of camaraderie and goodwill, as it is through a frame of support and mutual understanding that teachers and LSAs can work optimally in support of their students.

Chapter 4 considers the role of the LSA in responding to **challenging behaviour**. I consider several examples of challenging behaviour that LSAs may encounter over the course of their work, from rejection to work refusal and class avoidance. I underscore the need to put these forms of challenging behaviour into context, and to embrace modes of outside-the-box thinking in order to craft workable solutions that will best suit student needs. I highlight the importance of adopting a restorative approach to challenging behaviour, as LSAs are well placed to support their students to rebuild relationships with peers and teachers if things go wrong and become strained. I also consider a collaborative approach to behaviour management in the classroom, providing tips and insights for LSAs and teachers who wish to work together to address challenging behaviour. I additionally examine the role of the LSA as a mediator in this chapter, drawing on theories of conflict resolution to provide insight into the role of the LSA when it comes to solving issues and points of tension (Sellman et al., 2014). This chapter, in sum, examines numerous examples of challenging behaviour that LSAs may encounter over the course of their work, and I provide practical tips and reflective strategies to address them.

Chapter 5 underscores the importance of encouraging student **independence** as an LSA. I highlight the risks of the 'velcro LSA' (Skipp & Hopwood, 2019; Gerschel, 2005), and I provide numerous tips, techniques and strategies that LSAs can use to bolster student independence. In doing so, I consider certain barriers to student independence – as one LSA noted, 'it's all too easy to just slip into doing the work for them'. I focus particularly on reducing over-reliance when taking notes for students in class, and I suggest a range of methods – such as the check-in method, dual-working approaches and Cornell Notes (Pauk & Owens, 2010) – that LSAs can utilise to reduce pupil over-reliance. I additionally highlight the utility of in-class floating methods in this chapter, as such an approach can be used effectively to give a student pockets of independence over the course of their work during lessons. I note the importance of working with teachers to ensure optimal floating, and I consider the wider benefits of in-class LSA floating as they can enable a greater number of students to access academic support. I additionally highlight the importance of layering these methods with clear scaffolded roadmaps, in order to ensure that students are supported when pursuing a more independent approach to their learning. This chapter also underscores the importance of embracing pockets of silence and uncertainty as an LSA, and I consider the utility of reframing learning as a co-created practice between LSAs and students. I reaffirm the importance of respecting student autonomy and learning preferences in this chapter, as I have found that doing so marks a cornerstone of good LSA working practice. To this end, I provide tips for approaching learning conversations with students, to ensure that their voices are actively heard when discussing their preferred working dynamics with LSAs in class.

Chapter 6 re-examines the use of **dialogue** in LSA working practice. Drawing on the seminal work of Rupert Wegerif, I consider the central and largely under-examined role of dialogue in the work of LSAs. I introduce the idea that LSAs occupy quite a unique dialogic space given their liminal role within education, and that they have rich potential to use dialogue to co-create new and higher planes of understanding with students. I pay particular attention to the need for fertile dialogic spaces, as it is important for LSAs to encourage students to listen to the opinions of others and to exchange their views in a manner that is considerate and respectful of one another:

Introduction

> I think we're there to make sure that it stays respectful. There are some times when we have to say 'right, some people might have different opinions and that's OK'. And that's an important lesson for them to learn as well: that you're not going to agree with everybody you meet in life, especially in work life as well. So, it's important to know how to still be civil with these people and still get along with them, but you don't have to agree on everything.

I also examine the small pivots that LSAs could make to student dialogue in this chapter, providing tips and reflections for LSAs to encourage their students to consider a plurality of voices and perspectives within dialogue (Wegerif, 2017). I additionally emphasise the richness of the neurodivergent dialogic space, reflecting on many aspects of student dialogue that I have enjoyed over the course of my work as an LSA. This chapter fundamentally encourages LSAs to embrace dialogue as an academic process and end goal in and of itself, and I encourage LSAs to make intentional time for it over the course of their work with students in academic support departments. To this end, I examine numerous strategies that LSAs can utilise to foster dialogue with students – such as open-ended questions and think-aloud methods.

Chapter 7 explores the work of LSAs as it intersects with **assistive technology**. I consider the benefits of widely used educational technologies such as iPads and reader pens for student independence, foregrounding LSA views on the potential of such tech to enhance their working practice. This chapter also focuses on support for students with visual learning preferences, particularly when it comes to visual timetables, graphic novels and creative forms of doodle note-taking. I examine current innovations in the LSA working landscape, through an exploration of virtual reality and generative AI technologies that many LSAs are utilising to support student learning. I finally examine the utility of interdisciplinary learning support for students, reflecting on the ways in which LSAs can traverse the disciplines to build on pre-existing student strengths. I conclude with a reflection on the current junctures of LSA working practice in the age of AI, as I consider how the LSA role might adapt in the future in response to the current waves of technological innovation that we are witnessing as a society at present.

Chapter 8 reimagines the role of the LSA, as I chart positive **future changes** to LSA working lives and training opportunities moving forward. I begin by examining current gaps in the LSA training landscape, as I explore some of the barriers – such as high training loads and a lack of time and funding – that are limiting LSA access to training and further development opportunities. I consider individual LSA views on how their training could be improved, with a focus on scaffolding, support for high-ability students, future investment and greater access to professional SEND knowledge. I brainstorm potential future improvements to LSA training, articulating some ideas about a future qualification that could enhance both LSA skillsets and career progression opportunities. I highlight the importance of putting training into practice in this chapter, exploring the benefits for new starter LSAs of shadowing colleagues and observing student support sessions, to support a deeper understanding of the role. In this chapter, I additionally consider numerous challenges faced by LSAs – from low rates of pay to limited recognition and poor progression opportunities (Fazackerley, 2023; Hall & Webster, 2023; O'Brien & Garner, 2001), as these issues are contributing to recruitment and retention issues within the LSA profession (UNISON, 2022). I conclude by charting some potential solutions to these issues, citing LSA views and hopes when it comes to the direction of travel for their work in education moving forward.

These chapters have been designed to provide readers with tips, techniques and strategies to develop and refine their practice when it comes to student wellbeing, teacher relationships, challenging behaviour, learner independence, dialogue, assistive technology and training. I was careful to weave reflective questions throughout the book, inviting readers to consider how its core ideas might resonate with their working practice. I have been intentional about offering insights and ideas, as opposed to clear-cut answers, over the course of this work, as my experience has shown me that there cannot be a one-size-fits-all approach to the work of LSAs in education. Those in the SEND field who work closely with students each day will ultimately have invaluable grounded knowledge about what will work best for them in practice, and it is my ultimate hope that this book might offer some useful reflections – and indeed inspiration – along the way.

References

Education Endowment Foundation (EEF). (2021). *Making Best Use of Teaching Assistants: Guidance Report*. https://educationendowmentfoundation.org.uk/education-evidence/guidance-reports/teaching-assistants

Education & Training Foundation (ETF). (2019). *Learning Support Assistants in Further Education and Training: Guidance for Leaders and Managers*. www.et-foundation

.co.uk/document/learning-support-assistants-in-further-education-and-training-guidance-for-leaders-and-managers

Farrell, P., Balshaw, M., & Polat, F. (1999). *The Management, Role and Training of Learning Support Assistants*. DfEE Research Report No. 161. www.researchgate.net/publication/267936526_The_Management_Role_and_Training_of_Learning_Support_Assistants

Fazackerley, A. (May 14, 2023). Low pay 'forcing teaching assistants out of UK classrooms'. *The Guardian*. www.theguardian.com/education/2023/may/14/low-pay-teaching-assistants-uk-classrooms

Fox, G. (2003). *A Handbook for Learning Support Assistants: Teachers and Assistants Working Together*. David Fulton Publishers.

Gerschel, L. (2005). The special educational needs coordinator's role in managing teaching assistants: The Greenwich perspective. *Support for Learning 20*(2), 69–76. https://doi.org/10.1111/j.0268-2141.2005.00364.x

Gray, C., McCloy, S., Dunbar, C., Dunn, J., Mitchell, D., & Ferguson, J. (2007). Added value or a familiar face: The impact of learning support assistants on young readers. *Journal of Early Childhood Research, 5*(3), 285–300. https://doi.org/10.1177/1476718X07080474

Hall, S., & Webster, R. (2023). 'It's properly changed, and I think it's going to continue.' How the pandemic and the cost of living crisis remade the teaching assistant role. *Pastoral Care in Education 43*(1), 1–21. https://doi.org/10.1080/02643944.2023.2271483

McConkey, R., & Abbott, L. (2011). Meeting the professional needs of learning support assistants for pupils with complex needs. *Procedia Social and Behavioral Sciences 15*(2011) 1419–1424. https://doi.org/10.1016/j.sbspro.2011.03.305

Muijs, D., & Reynolds, D. (2003). The effectiveness of the use of learning support assistants in improving the mathematics achievement of low achieving pupils in primary school. *Educational Research 45*(3), 219–230. https://doi.org/10.1080/0013188032000137229

O'Brien, T., & Garner, P. (2001). *Untold Stories: Learning Support Assistants and Their Work*. Trentham Books.

Pauk, W., & Owens, R. (2010). *How to Study in College*. Cengage Learning.

Prince's Trust. (2022). *Class of Covid Report 2022*. https://downloads.ctfassets.net/qq0roodynp09/57AtHBpUjehEx5JWXsa5ma/59c709ea468ea6a95e4e71c644f6e40b/Class_of_Covid_Report_2022.pdf

Sellman, E., Cremin H., & McCluskey, G. (2014). *Restorative Approaches to Conflict in Schools: Interdisciplinary perspectives on whole school approaches to managing relationships*. Routledge.

Skipp, A., & Hopwood, V. (2019). *Deployment of Teaching Assistants in Schools: Research Report*. https://assets.publishing.service.gov.uk/media/5d1397fc40f0b6350e1ab56b/Deployment_of_teaching_assistants_report.pdf

UNISON. (2022). *School support staff cost-of-living survey 2022*. www.unison.org.uk/content/uploads/2022/11/UNISON-survey-for-Stars-22.pdf

Webster, R., & Blatchford, P. (2015). Worlds apart? The nature and quality of the educational experiences of pupils with a statement for special educational needs in mainstream primary schools. *British Educational Research Journal 41*(2), 324–342. https://doi.org/10.1002/berj.3144

Wegerif, R. (2017, September 5). Dialogic space and why we need it. [Rupert Wegerif]. www.rupertwegerif.name/blog/dialogic-space-why-we-need-it

Wright, N., Hill, J., Sharp, H., & Pickles, A. (2021). Interplay between long-term vulnerability and new risk: Young adolescent and maternal mental health immediately before and during the COVID-19 pandemic. *JCPP Advances 1*(1), e12008. https://doi.org/10.1111/jcv2.12008

1
Defining the LSA: what the LSA is (and isn't)

Chapter outline

Chapter 1 engages with a holistic definition of the LSA role. I reflect on:

- The LSA role as it relates to inclusive education
- The LSA/TA distinction
- Misconceptions surrounding the work of LSAs
- Hidden aspects of the role
- Key challenges facing LSAs
- Individual definitions of the role that are personal to LSAs
- LSA ethics of care and their views of education
- The importance of relationship building for LSAs
- Individual factors that can shape LSA working practice
- Navigating neurotypical expectations as an LSA

LSAs and educational inclusion

The LSA role has been strongly shaped by imperatives of inclusion for learners with additional needs (DfE & DHSC, 2014; Navarro, 2015). The scope of these additional learning requirements can vary hugely, but LSAs commonly work with students who have additional visual or hearing requirements, as well as students with autism, ADHD, dyslexia or those with specific social emotional and mental health (SEMH) needs such as anxiety. The crux of the LSA role concerns inclusion for learners with such additional learning requirements: LSAs support their students to fully participate in educational spaces and processes, and they are ultimately employed within education to ensure that their students can access their learning in a way that is optimal for them. Indeed, as one LSA noted:

I would define my role as facilitating the education of SEN students by ensuring that they have the same access to class resources, materials and opportunities as their peers. A fundamental part of my job is to ensure that a student comprehends what is required of them in class and that they have a sound understanding of what they are being taught. I would say that encouraging a student's sense of independence and self-reliance is also important.

It is interesting to note that despite the inclusive genesis of the role, it can sometimes be quite vague in its definition: 'there is no clear distinction between the work of LSAs with pupils with special educational needs (SEN) and that of other general classroom assistants' (Farrell et al., 1999, p.1). The work of LSAs can also fall under a range of titles within education, including, but not limited to, learning coaches, learning support mentors and learning support practitioners. Indeed, the boundaries of the LSA role can at times be quite fluid (Geeson & Clarke, 2022), and this has given rise to a growing imperative within the educational research landscape as of late for LSAs to avoid encroaching on the instructional role of teachers and to ensure that their students receive high levels of teacher interface and support (Breyer et al., 2021). The role is, moreover, largely context specific: no two students are the same, and the work of LSAs is often shaped by factors such as internal school cultures and the needs of individual students: 'It really depends on the culture of the place you're working at and also the students and the teachers you're working with.'

Although the role is largely context specific, common LSA duties and tasks include keeping pupils on task via 'prompting, acting as a scribe, explaining points, repeating instructions, checking the work pupils produce and helping them to correct their own mistakes' (Fox, 2003, p.8). Many LSAs also support students in navigating physical educational spaces by assisting with equipment such as wheelchairs, ramps and hoists ('We have one student I spent a lot of time with who has some mobility issues and so she might need help getting around the classroom, or some help with writing due to motor skills').

LSA tasks can vary across school types, with one participant from a primary school noting that their work often included things such as:

Helping all the children with their phonics, helping them outside, fixing up their knees if they fall over, doing first aid, talking to them about 'she doesn't want to be my best friend anymore', and also I've been doing a lot of covering for the teacher from time to time, so that includes teaching Maths, teaching PSHE, as well as covering lunchtime, reading, doing the register, telling stories and setting up what we're doing in the afternoon.

LSAs additionally have an important role to play when it comes to facilitating student access arrangements in accordance with JCQ regulations ('I spent two hours reading and scribing this morning, which at certain times of the year is actually a big part of the job').

My own experience of the role is that it has a strong pedagogical component, as I am often required to actively engage with student learning processes in order to provide optimal support in class. In practice, this might look like providing my student with a detailed checklist of steps to take to help them to approach a written task.

> **Top tip:** When writing task checklists, try not to overwhelm students with a lengthy list of steps – 'I think it's important to think about one or two goals to aim for as opposed to listing out a huge list for a student because then they could be overwhelmed, or might panic at the sight of it. I think if you set out two or three small steps for them to work on independently, you can start checking those off and then you can introduce new things.'

Sometimes I will also break a task down into smaller and more manageable components to make it more accessible for my students (task chunking). Often, I will provide them with research support guides to help them to approach key tasks (see Figure 1.1) and I frequently will provide things like brainstorming support and sentence starters to help them to begin with their work. My role as an LSA also has a focus on study skills: I run termly workshops where I provide students with revision and organisational support strategies, and I frequently work with individual students on a one-to-one basis to provide help with areas such as referencing, academic writing and deadline management.

> **Research Guide: Frida Kahlo**
>
> Consider Frida Kahlo's early life:
>
> - where was she born, and when?
> - What was her educational background like?
> - Was she born into a family of artists perhaps, did they support her work?
>
> Consider Kahlo's career and wider influences on her work:
>
> - Name the key milestones of her work: famous exhibitions, etc.
> - Did she win any awards?
> - What key events happened as she was completing her work – for example. war? Economic crisis, etc?
> - Do any of these key events impact her work in any way?
> - What were the cultural influences on her work?
>
> Key Kahlo Quotes:
>
> - Research what Kahlo has said:
> - What has she said about her art, her approach to her work?
> - What has she said about the variety of materials that she uses?
> - What does she consider to be the purpose of her work?
>
> Visual Analysis Research:
>
> - Note the key components of Kahlo's work:
> - Consider the colours she uses – what are the effects/symbolism of these colours?
> - Describe: media, shape, tone, line, etc
> - How do these pieces of art make the reader feel? What emotional responses do they provoke?
> - What is the aesthetic – the quality of the finish? Ie, how do colour, shape, texture, interrelate?
> - Discuss your personal views on her work

Figure 1.1 Research support guide

The role had a strong pedagogical focus for a learning coach I spoke with, who reflected on their work in supporting students to fill wider cultural knowledge gaps:

> Last year I worked with a girl, and she had pretty good English, but she didn't really have much cultural knowledge. So, I knew that going

into secondary school that she was going to have to be doing things like Shakespeare and poetry and literature, and that she was going to be at a disadvantage because of that. So, I worked with her and with another boy to plug some of those gaps of like who's the queen, who's Shakespeare, etc.

> Consider your own work as an LSA for a moment. What kind of tasks do you undertake to support the learning of your students?

Navigating the LSA/TA distinction: 'You're the bridge between the teacher and the kids'

In terms of the LSA/TA distinction, I remember that a former colleague of mine once reflected on the idea that 'the LSA supports the learner, and the TA supports the teacher'. Although many LSAs are very keen to support their teaching colleagues, it can be useful to do so in a balanced way that enables the LSA to remain attuned to the needs of their students in class.

> **Top tip:** Finding a 'gap' in class time may be the best way to navigate this, so LSAs can carve out some time to assist teachers once they have checked in with their student and ensured they are progressing well with their work. Keep in mind that an LSA's ability to assist a teacher will ultimately depend on student needs: if an LSA is required to take notes for a student with dyslexia, for example, then their scope to assist teachers may be more limited due to the demands of note-taking on their time.

The LSA role is unique in many ways, as it requires LSAs to engage with teachers and students and to build strong working relationships with both:

> A lot of people would define it as a step below a teacher, but I feel like it is a different thing altogether from a teacher because you're the bridge between the teacher and the kids. The old-school version

> would be that you're the assistant for the teacher, but you're not, you're sort of in the middle of both sides. So that's how I've always seen it – sometimes you're helping your kids communicate with the teacher, and other times it's helping the teacher communicate with the kids.

One learning coach I spoke to touched on this theme, and highlighted the value of the learning coach terminology in providing clarity when it came to their role and the scope of their work:

> Other people can use TAs more as like 'Could you go and photocopy these, could you stick those into the books?' [They can be treated] more as an assistant and I guess that's where the term 'teaching assistant' can maybe cause problems because it sounds like you're a PA or something and I don't think that's true anymore, not in the same way. I think it's why we're called learning coaches because I think early on that was recognised as maybe the wrong term to use and so the idea of being a learning coach (was coined). So, we're supporting the learning of the child: we're not supporting the teacher, we are here as a coach – we're here to help them learn, which I think is a subtle difference, but I think it's really important.

LSA misconceptions: 'I think the biggest [misconception] is that it's a mum job or that it's a nice easy nine-until-five kind of thing'

In addition to the TA/LSA conflation, broader misconceptions and assumptions can sometimes impact the work of LSAs in education. I have found that such misconceptions align with Miranda Fricker's concept of epistemic injustice: a process whereby one is wronged specifically in their capacity as a knower (Fricker, 2007). Much of the LSA interview data supports this view, as some of the LSAs I spoke with indicated that certain misconceptions clouded both their work and wider perceptions surrounding their knowledge, experience and skillsets. One participant shared that they felt they were seen as a 'tag-along' and another felt that they are seen as people who sat in class without working and following the lesson: 'They think that because you're in the class, you're not doing anything. My head is screwed on. I know what I'm doing.'

One participant I spoke with felt that it was often worth liaising with their colleagues to keep them in the loop about their qualifications and background experience:

> Actually, once you've spoken to [the colleague] and they've realised this person used to be an English teacher or that we've got [LSAs] here who've got PhDs – and it's almost like once teachers realise that this person used to be a teacher, or that they are very qualified, or that in their past life they were an engineer or something, then that shifts the dynamic slightly because I do think there is sometimes a bit of a stigma that TAs are just mums who want a job. I think there is that underlying feeling: not all people think that, but I do think there is a bit of that around.

In my view, such misconceptions are perhaps indicative of a lack of understanding of the LSA role within education, and they risk eclipsing the work that LSAs carry out in academic support departments in support of educational inclusion. Indeed, the overarching importance of the role is perhaps epitomised in the words of a former LSA, as they reflected on the idea that the role was unimportant within education:

> There are things that LSAs know and do that make a difference, because at the point when LSAs come, that's the peak of the individual's growth and learning – all that brain energy is firing, and if you prop them up there, they can go on to do great, but if you push them down, they're going to be stuck in that bubble for a long time. So, I think there's a misconception that LSAs aren't important, which is very much not true.

Despite certain misconceptions surrounding the role, LSAs often draw on a highly skilled knowledge base to support their students. This knowledge base is often both practical and academic: many LSAs have valuable lived experience of caring for neurodivergent family members, whilst others are often graduates with diverse disciplinary backgrounds. The diverse knowledge base of LSAs was indeed reflected in the interview sample that underpins this book: one participant I spoke with had eight years of SEND experience working as an LSA, another had a degree in Special Educational Needs, and I additionally interviewed an LSA who was a qualified English as an additional language (EAL) teacher.

I have a degree in education, which I have often found to be very useful over the course of my work as an LSA. It is also worth bearing in mind that many LSAs can feel highly valued and appreciated by their colleagues:

> A lot of the teachers that I've worked with are absolutely amazing with the students that we support. Sometimes they'll take multiple times out of their lessons just to walk over and say, 'Are you doing all right?' or 'Do you need help with anything?' They'll say, 'I've done this for you, can you make sure that it's all right?' And then they'll show me the paper or whatever they're doing and then they'll confirm whether it's all right or they'll let me go around the class and help other people.

Indeed, research indicates that 'teachers generally value the contribution that learning support staff make to teaching and learning' (Navarro, 2015, p.38) and this is something I have personally found to be the case over the course of my work in the sixth form sector, as my colleagues often take time to check in with me during lessons, frequently thanking me for my efforts in in supporting students.

There's more to the LSA than meets the eye: 'You're the one that's creating the strength and the resilience for them to go forward. It's more than just supporting a student with their work'

LSAs, as I have discussed so far, perform a range of academic tasks to support students in fully accessing their learning. There is often more to the role than meets the eye, however, as lots of LSAs carry out additional forms of pastoral and socialisation support that can be harder to notice within education: 'We all do those extra bits, whether it's just because they're upset and they've asked you to listen to them and solve their friendship problems, so you talk it through.' The role is highly supportive and pastoral in nature, with many LSAs working closely with students to overcome barriers and to boost their self-esteem and self-concept within education:

> The role of an LSA is misunderstood by many and it's incredibly important. We mould a student's life as much as a teacher does, if not more so because of the amount of time you spend with someone

Defining the LSA: what the LSA is (and isn't)

in a one-to-one working situation. You're the one that's creating the strength and the resilience for them to go forward. It's more than just supporting a student with their work.

Indeed, for one LSA, the role was underpinned by an advanced form of problem solving: 'That's what an LSA is. It's advanced problem solving because you are thinking on your toes the entire time.' This idea was echoed by a former LSM that I spoke to, who noted that LSAs had to think on their feet very frequently in education to process key information:

You have to hear information, process it quicker than anyone else in the room, pass it on in a way that it can be processed [by the student] and all in a space of time where most people in that room are just about picking up their pens and getting on with stuff. It's not an easy task by any means.

These insights resonate strongly with my experience of working as an LSA, and they align interestingly with the idea of moment-to-moment pedagogy – Paju and colleagues (2016) described that school assistants get used to adapting to varying situations, which can be called 'moment-to-moment pedagogy' (Paju et al., 2016, as cited in Sirkko et al., 2022, p.2768).

LSAs also have an important role to play when it comes to facilitating enrichment activities and social skills support for students: 'We've got a chit chat group, and my colleague runs a games group. So, via all these other groups, we do teach them social interaction and social skills.' Many of my colleagues also run clubs during lunch times to give students the chance to access safe spaces in college whilst engaging with fun activities such as playing the Nintendo Switch and watching weekly films. I have also found that socialisation support marks an important aspect of my role as an LSA. My colleagues and I are cognisant of the need to model pro-social behaviours and general pleasantries within our department – such as conversational turn-taking, active listening, polite greetings, cordial conversations with colleagues, etc – in support of the life skills of our students.

LSAs also have a key role to play in encouraging social engagement between students and their peers. The LSA can be an effective 'bridge' in this respect, perhaps by inviting students to engage in dialogue with one another, or to participate in more structured social activities such as chess or card games if they have a gap in their timetable. Indeed, one HLTA I spoke to used a social prompt strategy to help their students to build connections with their peers in primary school contexts:

> Some children that I work with find the social interaction side really quite challenging. So, we've been [facilitating] friendship groups where you give the children little sentence stems to help them start a conversation with someone. So, we'll be playing a game, and you could say something like 'It's your turn now' or 'You're doing really well, I'm really happy for you'.

LSAs, in sum, provide a plethora of support to students that does not necessarily meet the eye in education: 'For me, it was a much broader thing than just the academic support.' This is particularly true when supporting students with anxiety as it may seem, at first glance, that the LSA isn't doing much in support of their student when their presence in the lesson itself can provide support and encouragement to students who may otherwise struggle to access their learning.

> Consider your own work as an LSA for a moment. Can you think of any 'hidden' aspects of your role that you would like to be more widely acknowledged?

LSA working challenges: from high workloads to subject confidence and a lack of understanding

The LSAs that I interviewed for this book identified a plethora of challenges that shaped their working lives, including:

- Workload
- School hierarchies
- Accessing materials and resources
- Subject confidence
- The mental load of working as an LSA
- Limited recognition

Workload was identified as a key challenge: LSAs often have to balance break and lunch duties, admin tasks and record-keeping responsibilities alongside their daily classroom commitments. As one participant put it: 'There just isn't enough hours in the day to try and get everything done.' Schools are witnessing increasing numbers of students with additional support needs, many of whom do not have EHCPs, and this current working context can present further challenges for LSAs as it can be difficult to provide in-class academic support to increasing numbers of students: '[This was] really challenging because you've got about ten students who [are struggling with the work], and you're trying to get through them all.'

> **Top tip:** Liaising with teachers can be a good way of navigating this challenge as an LSA as one LSA noted that 'sometimes I might even say to the teacher "there's quite a few of them that are (struggling with) this. Can you maybe go over it a different way?" And so then the teacher can get the whole class and go "right, let's recap this, let's try and look at this a different way".' Adopting a group-based approach to in-class support, where you float across different groups depending on the levels of need, might also be a good solution when it comes to supporting multiple students in a single classroom setting.

In addition to issues of workload, schools can be quite hierarchical and stratified working environments (Watson et al., 2013). Indeed, for one LSA, navigating a sense of division posed a challenge to their work as they felt that 'sometimes in some schools there can be a real "us and them" culture between teachers and the LSA'. Tips for navigating such challenges – and building an optimal teacher–LSA liaising relationship – will be examined in further detail in Chapter 3. In addition to a sense of division between teachers and LSAs, it can sometimes be challenging for LSAs to speak up when they require access to certain materials. It can be awkward to request things such as a seat in a lesson if one hasn't been provided, and some LSAs may feel uneasy about requesting access to materials and resources in class. One LSA noted during an interview that 'for English they happen to have a spare poetry anthology, so I make notes in that'. Although some LSAs have access to in-class resources, these materials aren't always readily available.

> **Top tip:** It's a good idea to collaborate with teachers to navigate some of these challenges and to communicate directly about your in-class requirements as an LSA (see Chapter 3 for more details).

For many LSAs, a challenge of the role can cluster around subject confidence, as it can often be quite difficult initially to support a student in a subject that you are not familiar with:

> The issue of subject confidence with LSAs is another one. I don't really know how you solve that because, by definition, even if they have knowledge of one subject, they can't have it for all the classes that they're in.

I have certainly found this to be the case, as I have discovered that it's much easier to support my students with subjects that I have direct knowledge of – such as Sociology – as I am already familiar with most of the fundamental theories and concepts that underpin the A Level.

> **Top tip:** It's a good idea to check in with your line manager about this, and to perhaps suggest a subject allocation meeting at the beginning of the academic year as you are finalising LSA timetables. Audit the backgrounds and skillsets of your LSA colleagues, to ascertain who is most confident to work across each subject area: once you have identified these preferences, try to weave them into the timetable accordingly. It might be a good idea to review this quarterly, to ensure the LSAs in your team are happy with their subject caseloads.

One LSA additionally noted that a challenge of the role stemmed from the fact that it could at times be mentally draining and quite un-engaging:

> I much prefer the pastoral side where I am working one to one with a student. I think sitting in other people's lessons for more than a few

more years would drive me bonkers, and it's not because it's not worthwhile but it's not active enough for a start.

For this LSA, however, a solution lay in diversifying their daily activities as much as possible over the course of their work:

> Luckily, the bit I've been given more to do is working one to one, mentoring students, and I feel that is much more productive. And I've worked on things like organisational skills, I run sessions on things like essay planning. I've used a lot of the critical thinking skills that I've got with helping students and I have worked with students one to one as a mentor. I think in some ways I find it more rewarding and it's possibly more productive than being in so many classrooms.

I have also found it useful to diversify my work week with activities such as group study skills workshops, as it makes a refreshing change from attending a weekly loop of lessons.

One LSA I spoke with felt that the challenges of the role often weren't acknowledged in education, reflecting that:

> I think sometimes there isn't the recognition of what a tough job it is. Every day you have to bring your A Game. You have to forget what happened yesterday because you're in very close proximity and you have to forget rejection and the things that happened yesterday and start every day with a clean slate. I think sometimes people are not aware of how hard that is because if you're in a lesson that's a disaster, you'll still with that one to one for the next lesson – you have to pick them back up and say 'OK, Maths was a disaster today, but now we've got English!' The Maths teacher has gone but you're still there.

Individual LSA definitions: 'An LSA is someone that supports the student to ensure that they achieve their full potential while also encouraging their own independence for the future'

Despite the challenges that come alongside the role, many LSAs are highly committed to their work and remain deeply passionate about it. This sense of commitment was palpable throughout the conversations I had with LSAs, as we discussed what the role meant to them on a more personal level. For one former LSA, the essence of the role clustered around the idea of equity:

> I suppose if you look at it in terms of equality and **equity** – everyone else is able to see over the fence and you (as an LSA) are essentially that box that they will stand on top of to also see over the fence.

For another LSA, the idea of **service** to others was central: '[Being an LSA means] giving something back to the community – just to make sure that [students] get enough help so that they can succeed.'

Advocacy was key to the role for one TSA I spoke with:

> It means being an advocate for your student: making sure they've got what they want and what they need, making sure that all the things in the background are done so that exam referrals are done, learning support interviews are done and that the teachers have access to full EHCPs.

The idea of holistic support was central to the role for one HLTA, who reflected:

> You do a million different things throughout the day – you're a nurse, you're an educator and you're also that support network for the teacher that you work with, but you're also somebody who's providing all that wrap-around emotional care for the students that you work with as well.

For others, the role can have a more **personal** meaning. One participant I spoke to had received LSA support at sixth form, and stepping into the role themselves marked a way of giving back to their community:

> I think in terms of what it means to me, I became an LSA because the learning support was the main thing that drew me to it. Because having an LSA when I was a student was paramount to me doing well, I think, in my final History exam specifically. So, I enjoyed receiving that. So, I wanted to give it a go as well because I think it's so rewarding when you feel like you've helped someone, and you feel like you're putting that knowledge to good use.

The role was intrinsically motivational for another participant I spoke with, as a core element of their work centred around inspiring the next generation of students to appreciate the value of education and its opportunities:

> I am an influencer, motivator and advocate. My role as an LSA is to advocate for my students, liaise with others to ensure that I have removed the barriers to their learning for that session. I'm a role model, a sounding board, a person who is respected once I know how to give space and accept their shortcomings. I have high expectations of myself and my students. I want to fill them with motivation and confidence. **I want to inspire them** and to let them know that education can take them places, like it did with me. It is the key to success.

Indeed, for another LSA, fostering student **independence** was key to their definition of their work:

> It's different with every student but I think it's about enabling students to access the curriculum in a way that they wouldn't necessarily be able to without support. So, it's definitely not doing things for them, but especially in secondary school, it's about encouraging independent learning, and helping them towards that independence.

This focus on student independence resonates with what a former colleague once told me about the role as they likened the LSA to training wheels on a bike: they are there for support, but it is ultimately the student who has to pedal.

This LSA role, in sum, has rich and insightful meanings that are unique to each of the individuals that work in it. Indeed, some of these are structured around:

- Equity
- Serving the community
- Advocacy
- Caring for students
- Motivating young people
- Supporting student independence

> Consider your own work as an LSA for a moment. What does the role mean to you, on a personal level? What inspired you to pursue your work as an LSA?

LSA ethics of care and a holistic view of education

In addition to individual LSA definitions of their role, overarching questions of education and its purpose can shape core LSA conceptualisations of their role. LSAs touched upon holistic ideas of education, as many noted that it transcended the purely academic realm. One former LSA that I interviewed directly commented on this idea, by remarking that 'education isn't just academic: its **social**; you find out more about how to make friends, negotiation, even if it's about playtime and sharing and how to be good'.

For another participant, a fundamental aspect of their role concerned the welfare of their students and their development as people: 'In the class [you need to ensure that] the students are happy because unhappy kids don't learn.' For this TSA, the crux of their role wasn't solely academic as they were concerned with the **character development** of their students: 'For me it's not all about learning anyway, it's kind of 50% learning and 50% who they are if that makes any sense.' Indeed, a core aspect of their work was concerned with building safe spaces where students could truly be themselves in an environment that supported both epistemic humility and not knowing: 'I think it's all about creating an environment where it's safe to be yourself and it's safe not to know.'

In addition to a holistic view of the purpose of education, many LSAs structured their work around an ethic of care and support for their students. For one participant, the purpose of their role was to **uplift** their students, as they aimed to inspire and support them: 'If I can make one kid happy within themselves, I'll achieve something in my job.' They specifically highlighted that LSAs should 'tell children they're special and important because a lot of teachers don't say that to students, and they don't get told that – it's a big thing.'

Another participant's ethic of care was structured around providing support for student **welfare**: 'The most important thing as an LSA isn't to help them learn. It's to keep them safe.' For them, part of supporting student welfare meant building a safe space for students so that 'when they do want to speak to you, they know that you're there for them'.

A further ethic of care was articulated by an LSA who reflected on their role and stated: 'I think being an LSA means you're there for the children, you're there so they can approach you and you can help them in any way that they want, and they need.' For this LSA, their ethic of care and **kindness** was inspired by a personal experience as they shared that they had a child with dyslexia who had not been supported optimally within education. They reflected that 'having had that experience as a parent, perhaps that made me more aware of (the need to be) kind to children who have disabilities'.

These insights from LSAs outline their personal ethics of care and their overarching conceptualisations of education, reflecting important yet perhaps under-examined dimensions of the LSA role.

The LSA and relationship building: 'Each student is different and needs to be "read" individually as you go along. What works for one may not work for another'

For one LSA, the essence of their work clustered around relationship building with individual students: 'I think you've just got to build up a relationship with them to get it to work.' This insight touches on the idea that there is no one-size-fits-all approach to working as an LSA. Although there are clear guidance and parameters for good working practice (EEF, 2021; Breyer et al., 2021), there is not necessarily a set formula that underpins a successful student/LSA working dynamic. I have found in my experience that 'what works' with each student will often become clear over time, as you get to know them and their individual ways of being. In many ways, a successful LSA will be able to read situations at pace, ascertaining what a student needs and presenting it to them in a supportive and constructive manner:

> You need to be a magician and therapist and teacher and God all rolled into one. You need to be able to be whatever a situation needs as you are supporting a student. You need to be somebody who is able to do that.

The role is largely rooted in **connection** ('you're a safe person that they can connect to'), and I have found that the one-to-one nature of the work will often help LSAs to build strong and supportive educational relationships with their students.

Indeed, another LSA reflected on the essence of the role and noted that it was largely **iterative** in nature:

> You can think of yourself a bit like a sculptor and every student is your raw material, and your job is to see the potential in that raw material. But it's very much an iterative process, the only way of finding out what is in that raw material is going through the process of working with them. It's a bit like a craftsperson or an artist. You've got to have a palette of colours and skills which you can develop and rehearse and think through and have stored. But actually, pulling the right one out at the right moment, that is the art of the thing.

Each of these insights resonates with my experience of working as an LSA, and the ultimate tip I would give to others in similar roles would be to get to know your students: spend time chatting with them, find out what they like and draw on those interests to build a rapport with them. Be patient, trust the process of working together and have faith in your own knowledge as an LSA: over time, you will be able to identify what works and what doesn't.

> Consider your own work as an LSA for a moment. Do any of these insights ring true in your experience? How might you navigate the journey of finding 'what works' when supporting individual students?

From academic grounding to personal motivations: what factors might shape the LSA working craft?

Although there is no one-size-fits-all approach to LSA working practice, I have found that there is value in considering the underlying factors and even assumptions that have come to shape my craft as an LSA. This frame of personal reflection has enabled me to scrutinise and consider the core elements of my work, and the extent to which I might refine them for future improvement. I was struck when interviewing one LSA that a fundamental element of their outlook towards the role had been shaped by a personal experience: their own child with dyslexia had not been treated optimally within education, and this experience cemented their awareness of the need to approach the LSA role with a fundamental sense of **compassion**.

In a similar vein, my own approach to working as an LSA was shaped strongly by my undergraduate studies. I spent three years studying pedagogy and the essence of learning as part of my education degree at Homerton College. I spent a large chunk of time reflecting on what education was as a phenomenon in and of itself, and it was through this line of thinking that I became interested in dialogue as a process that is fundamental to our existence in the world and our ability to bring knowledge into being. This grounding in dialogic education theory, which I gained thanks to attending some lectures taught by Rupert Wegerif, influenced me to adopt a **dialogic approach** to my work as an LSA. From an early point in my practice, I was keen to facilitate engaging dialogic spaces for my students – where they could examine ideas, explore diverse viewpoints and question their own assumptions and those of others. Often, this required me to probe and gently challenge, in the interests of enabling reflective conversation (see Chapter 6 for more details on the use of dialogue for LSAs). Frequently, it required me to listen attentively, enabling my students to develop skills of oratory and articulation as they vocalised their opinions and views about the world. It was important to me that they should feel heard and valued within the dialogic space, safe in the knowledge that their views mattered and that I as an LSA was there to listen.

My own LSA craft (which I am consciously refining and developing) can thus be described as quite dialogic. On a practical level, this often results in conversations with my students where we discuss their ideas, focusing on how and why they know things in order to support their epistemic – or knowledge-based – frames. This approach to working as an LSA remains unique to me, and it was shaped strongly by contextual factors such as my studies at Homerton and my interest in dialogue. I feel, in many ways, that my personal approach to working as an LSA reflects something beautiful about the profession: LSAs – whilst remaining true to the guidelines of good practice (EEF, 2021) – have the autonomy to mould their craft in a way that fulfils and interests them individually.

> Consider your own work as an LSA for a moment in light of this chapter. What factors might have shaped your individual craft? Could your practice have been shaped by the influence of a particular academic discipline? Or might your work have been shaped by a more personal motivation that stems from the lived experience of caring for a person with additional learning needs?

Stepping into a student's frame of reference – navigating neurotypical expectations in a neurodiverse field: 'For me, I have to get into their mindset, rather than my own mindset'

I have, finally, found it useful to reflect on my own neurotypical expectations when it comes to my work as an LSA. LSAs frequently work with students who are members of the neurodivergent community. The concept of neurodiversity is highly relevant to the work of LSAs:

> [F]rom a neurodiversity perspective, the differences in the way people perceive, learn about and interact with the world are conceptualised as naturally occurring cognitive variation, akin to biodiversity in the natural environment, which may bring unique strengths and challenges for individuals.
>
> (Hamilton & Petty, 2023, p.1)

Although many LSAs can themselves have neurodivergent ways of processing the world, it is useful to consider the extent to which LSAs may sometimes bring 'neurotypical' assumptions to their practice. I have certainly found this to be the case over the course of my work as an LSA, and I felt it would be useful to briefly consider this theme to provide some reflective insights into what such a 'perspective clash' may look like in practice. I once remember, in the early days of my practice, observing that a student didn't seem to have many peers to chat with at lunchtime. I was concerned they may be experiencing loneliness, and so I brought it up in conversation with a colleague. This colleague in question had extensive SEND knowledge and helped me to appreciate that social connections may look slightly different for that individual. Over the course of our discussion, she helped me to see that I had, in fact, projected a neurotypical assumption ('they must be lonely') on to the student in question. So too has this happened when it comes to dealing with forms of what may seem like 'attention-seeking' behaviour from students. I once discussed this with my manager, who helped me to appreciate that such behaviour was, in fact, much better conceptualised as being 'attachment seeking' (NSPCC Learning, 2023, Inclusive Teach, 2023).

It is worth bearing in mind that it can be normal to make these types of 'errors' as an LSA: we all approach the world through unique and contextual lenses, and it can often take time to appreciate the deeper nuances that are integral to working in the SEND field. What's important is to remain open to learning: I spoke to more experienced colleagues about these assumptions when they occurred over the course of my work, and they used their knowledge to help me see things from a different – and more informed and empathetic – perspective. These forms of reflexive thinking are perhaps useful to cultivate as an LSA, as is a frame of compassionate understanding which is 'termed *cognitive empathy*: trying to understand the students' situation, take on their perspectives, and understand their thoughts, motivations, and motives' (Cerbin and Kopp, 2006, as cited in Aas et al., 2023, p.68).

> Consider your own work as an LSA for a moment. Have you ever had an experience where you have viewed a situation from a neurotypical perspective? What steps might you take in the future to support a more empathetic approach to your working practice?

Concluding reflections

Over the course of this chapter, I have sought to define the work of LSAs in broad and holistic terms, exploring aspects of the role that are often underexamined within education. The work of LSAs is structured around core imperatives of educational inclusion, yet I have also found that foundational ethics of care often lie at the heart of the role. Individual relationships with students are integral to the work of LSAs, and one participant that I spoke with was insightful in their reflection that 'each student is different, and needs to be "read" individually as you go along. What works for one may not work for another.' LSAs also apply richly personal meanings to their work

– glimmers of which have been explored in this chapter – and I hope I may have prompted readers to consider the role and its essence on a deeper level, in light of all that underpins it.

> Consider your own work as an LSA for a moment. How might the role be optimally defined, in your view?

References

Aas, H. K., Uthus, M., & Løhre, A. (2023). Inclusive education for students with challenging behaviour: Development of teachers' beliefs and ideas for adaptations through Lesson Study. *European Journal of Special Needs Education* 39(1), 64–78. https://doi.org/10.1080/08856257.2023.2191107

Breyer, C., Lederer, J., & Gasteiger-Klicpera, B. (2021). Learning and support assistants in inclusive education: A transnational analysis of assistance services in Europe. *European Journal of Special Needs Education* 36(3), 344–357. https://doi.org/10.1080/08856257.2020.1754546

Cerbin, W., & Kopp, B. (2006). Lesson Study as a Model for Building Pedagogical Knowledge and Improving Teaching. *International Journal of Teaching and Learning in Higher Education* 18(3), 250–257. www.isetl.org/ijtlhe

Department for Education (DfE) and Department for Health and Social Care (DHSC). (2014). *Statutory guidance. SEND code of practice: 0 to 25 years.* www.gov.uk/government/publications/send-code-of-practice-0-to-25

Education Endowment Foundation (EEF). (2021). *Making Best Use of Teaching Assistants: Guidance Report.* https://educationendowmentfoundation.org.uk/education-evidence/guidance-reports/teaching-assistants

Farrell, P., Balshaw, M., & Polat, F. (1999). *The Management, Role and Training of Learning Support Assistants.* DfEE Research Report No. 161. www.researchgate.net/publication/267936526_The_Management_Role_and_Training_of_Learning_Support_Assistants

Fox, G. (2003). *A Handbook for Learning Support Assistants: Teachers and Assistants Working Together.* David Fulton Publishers.

Fricker, M. (2007). *Epistemic Injustice: Power and the Ethics of Knowing.* Oxford University Press.

Geeson, R., & Clarke, E. (2022). Crossing the line: Constructs of TA identity. *Pastoral Care in Education* 41(2), 245–261. https://doi.org/10.1080/02643944.2022.2032813

Hamilton, L, G., & Petty, S. (2023). Compassionate pedagogy for neurodiversity in higher education: A conceptual analysis. *Frontiers in Psychology* 14, 1093290. https://doi.org/10.3389/fpsyg.2023.1093290

Inclusive Teach: Special Education and Inclusive Learning. (2023, June 6). Attachment and Attention-Seeking Behaviour in Young Children. https://inclusiveteach.com/2023/06/06/attachment-and-attention-seeking-behaviour-in-young-children-understanding-the-connection

Navarro, M. F. (2015). Learning support staff: A literature review. OECD Education Working Paper No. 125. https://doi.org/10.1787/5jrnzm39w45l-en

NSPCC Learning. (2023, February 24). Why language matters: in need of attention, not 'attention seeking'. https://learning.nspcc.org.uk/news/why-language-matters/in-need-of-attention-not-attention-seeking

Paju, B., Räty, L., Pirttimaa, R., & Kontu, E. (2016). The school staff's perception of their ability to teach pupils with special educational needs in inclusive settings in Finland. *International Journal of Inclusive Education 20*(8), 801–815. https://doi.org/10.1080/13603116.2015.1074731

Sirkko, R., Sutela, K., & Takala, M. (2022). School assistants' experiences of belonging. *International Journal of Inclusive Education 28*(12), 2765–2781. https://doi.org/10.1080/13603116.2022.2122607

Watson, D., Bayliss, P., & Pratchett, G. (2013). Pond life that 'know their place': Exploring teaching and learning support assistants' experiences through positioning theory. *International Journal of Qualitative Studies in Education 26*(1), 100–117. https://doi.org/10.1080/09518398.2011.598195

2
The LSA and wellbeing support

Chapter outline

Chapter 2 examines the role of LSAs in providing wellbeing support to students. I discuss:

- The central role of wellbeing support in the work of LSAs
- Specific LSA safeguarding considerations
- Signposting tips for LSAs
- Professional boundaries as an LSA
- Active listening
- Little chats and small check-ins
- Gentle assertiveness, encouraging rest breaks, providing reeassurance and never judging
- LSA motivational techniques
- Nature and wellbeing
- LSA wellbeing tips

The centrality of wellbeing support to the work of LSAs: 'Unhappy kids don't learn'

Wellbeing and pastoral support are intrinsic to the work of LSAs (Hall & Webster, 2023). This was particularly true for one participant I spoke with, who reflected on their work in giving reassurance and emotional support to primary school students:

> For the reception children when they start, it's a massive thing for them, it's their first time at school. There is often lots of tears and you are the familiar face to talk to them every day, to guide them, to help

them with their coat, to make sure that they're OK. You sit with them and tell them stories if they need it, and you make sure that they're OK. There is also support for physical wellbeing and lots of reassurance and making sure that they're safe and they know that they can tell you anything.

The wellbeing of students can significantly impact their academic progression (Bauld, 2021), and I have found over the course of my work as an LSA that it is integral to actively support the wellbeing and happiness of my students – this aspect of the LSA role is particularly important given that some students with SEND may experience high rates of depression (Van Heijst et al., 2020). Wellbeing, broadly speaking, concerns 'how people feel and how they function, both on a personal and a social level, and how they evaluate their lives as a whole' (New Economics Forum, 2012, p.6). The wellbeing of young people can be shaped strongly by their social connections – for a group of Samoan children, for example, wellbeing meant connecting with loved ones, not having to worry, being a good person, feeling valued and included, and having a sense of belonging (Dunlop-Bennett et al., 2019, p.109). Having a sense of purpose, and feeling as if your work has meaning, is also very important in supporting wellbeing and human flourishing (O'Brien & Guiney, 2021).

Wellbeing will likely have a subjective meaning for each student; however, being well in education might mean that a young person connects with the intrinsic value of their work: they may experience a state of creative flow as they work on a design project, for example, or they might feel a sense of happiness and joy as they enjoy spending time with their friends. Wellbeing is shaped strongly by material factors, and it is vital that students feel comfortable and safe in their homes and that they have access to plentiful and nutritious meals as they progress throughout their educational journeys and their lives more broadly (Garvie et al., 2023; Firth et al., 2020). Being well also connects strongly with being free from fear – particularly fear of violence and bullying (Cremin & Guilherme, 2015). Access to supportive networks is integral to the wellbeing of young people, and I have found that LSAs have a very important role to play in academic support departments in building an overarching culture of care and inclusion, where students feel safe to speak about things that may be worrying them in their lives. The wellbeing components of the role resonated strongly with one LSA I spoke to, who reflected:

> I feel that wellbeing needs to come before the education part simply because if a student isn't comfortable or feeling too great in any way, shape or form, then they're not going to produce to the best of their ability academically. So, wellbeing is very important and vital to their education.

Students are, moreover, facing a plethora of wellbeing challenges which have only been compounded by events such as the Covid-19 pandemic and the cost-of-living crisis. Recent PISA research found that a high number of UK teenagers are skipping meals due to poverty-related factors (McSorley et al., 2023), and years of Covid-induced educational disruption and fragmented social interaction have contributed to rising cases of depression and anxiety among students (Norwich et al., 2022; Wright et al., 2021; Prince's Trust, 2022). Pupil loneliness and exam stress are additionally impacting the educational experiences of young people, as are chronic issues such as cyberbullying, self-harm and eating disorders (ONS, 2020; Twenge et al, 2021; Trafford et al., 2023). The pupil wellbeing landscape of schools and FE colleges across the UK has become increasingly challenging in recent years, and it is in this context that LSAs have an important role to play in supporting the wellbeing of students.

The LSA and safeguarding

The work of LSAs comes with some specific safeguarding considerations. Students with SEND are at a higher risk of abuse and neglect than their peers (Safeguarding Network, 2024), and it is therefore important for LSAs to remain attuned to warning signs which could indicate that their student is at risk. Keep in mind that LSAs have what is akin to a unique safeguarding vantage point in education: they often spend extended periods of time with students and will likely have the opportunity to check in with them daily to see how they are doing. LSAs often sit with them in lessons and can thus be well placed to pick up on small details about student behaviour and appearance that could otherwise go unnoticed ('in terms of every day we're the front line'). As an LSA, you will know your students well: be attuned to any changes in their behaviour and don't hesitate to share your concerns with your safeguarding team. Keep in mind that every detail matters when it comes to safeguarding – even a small observation from an LSA could help your safeguarding team to contextualise an issue or pinpoint a pattern of behaviour, and it is always important to log a safeguarding report if you have concerns.

> **Top tip:** Keep in mind that sharing and logging safeguarding concerns will take priority over your daily academic tasks. Don't hesitate to stop what you are doing and go into a quieter working environment if you need to report a safeguarding concern. It's also important to keep tabs on any unexplained student absences. You will often be the first person on the front line to notice that your student is not present, and it's always worth following up with them to double check that they are okay. I typically inform a specialist teacher if I notice that my student is not in their lesson, as they will be able to investigate further and get in contact with the student if needs be.

I have found as an LSA that it's important to have open dialogue with your students about safeguarding. Let them know that it's your job to keep them safe, and that you will always follow up with members of your safeguarding team if you feel there is an area of concern. Never promise to withhold information or to keep anything they tell you secret, in recognition of the fact that sharing such information is an integral aspect of a safe educational environment. Keep in mind that your job as an LSA is to build a supportive relationship with your student, where they feel they can let you know if something isn't right: 'There's a kind of safeguarding element, I think as well, with making sure that they know that they're safe so that they can then tell you anything, talk about anything that's bothering them and see a friendly face.'

> Consider your own work as an LSA for a moment. How might you best use your position as an LSA to protect the wellbeing and safety of your students?

Signposting as an LSA

I have sometimes found it useful to reflect on the parameters of my role as an LSA and to acknowledge my own limitations: whilst many LSAs may have mental health first-aid training, they are not fully qualified mental health professionals, and it is therefore really important to be mindful of not overstepping the mark when providing wellbeing support to students. General discussion around how a student is doing can be very constructive; however, more professional conversations concerning the need for a diagnosis, or why students are experiencing certain thoughts or feelings, should be left for mental health professionals. In order to optimally support and signpost students, it is good practice for LSAs to familiarise themselves with the professional sources of support that are available within their educational institutions and wider communities.

> **Top tip:** Print wellbeing cards that detail key sources of support and leave some in your working space so they can be easily accessed should you need them for signposting. You could also attach some laminated copies to your lanyard or keep some in your notebook, so they are easily accessible!

Liaising with colleagues and wider professional sources of support is another key component of student wellbeing support, as it can help students to access specialist help should they need it. One participant I spoke to reflected on this:

> I was supporting a little boy whose dad had passed away. He had lots of difficulties expressing his feelings and I found that particularly tricky, that was quite a difficult time because I felt like I wasn't always the right person to work with him because I was finding those conversations difficult to have myself. So, in the end I spoke to the SENCO about it and said, I think that he also needs extra support in this area because there's some things that I don't feel comfortable talking about [due to some personal circumstances]. In the end, they referred him to counselling – he still had that support in class with me, so if he did

want to speak to anybody, he could speak to me or the teacher, but the school also brought in extra counselling for him. So then, that way, that whole pressure wasn't on me – the school were really supportive.

The importance of liaising with colleagues to support student wellbeing was echoed by another LSA, who reflected on what that process would look like in their educational context:

We have student progress managers and they basically are the person you liaise with on each site about each student. I think the best way to support those students would be if they say anything, if they're worried about anything, I just go, "well I'll mention it to [the progress manager]" because at the end of the day, they are going to be the people who can put things in place.

These anecdotes indicate the importance of signposting as an LSA, highlighting the benefits of liaising with co-workers and wider professionals in support of student wellbeing. I have found it's useful for LSAs to build relationships with colleagues such as safeguarders, counsellors, wellbeing coordinators and student pastoral/progress managers so they can work alongside them to enhance student welfare in education. Open dialogue is really important when supporting students, so try to keep these key people in the loop as much as you can – scheduling a termly check-in might be helpful here, so people have the chance to meet in person to discuss student support.

Professional boundaries as an LSA: 'You're not the student's mate; you are in a professional role with them'

In addition to signposting considerations, it is worth reflecting on maintaining professional boundaries as an LSA. The need to establish these boundaries between students and LSAs stems from the fact that LSAs work within a liminal educational space: they are not a teacher, yet they are also not a student. LSAs will attend lessons alongside their students, and many will access the same shared spaces in academic support departments. Considering these working dynamics, some students may be inclined to view the LSA as a peer as opposed to a professional member of staff. I have found it useful in these cases for LSAs to be very clear around the scope of their role, and it is a good rule of thumb to have clear and open dialogue to establish the boundaries between LSAs and students: 'You're not the student's mate, you are in a professional role with them.'

I remember once hearing a student use the word 'mate' when referring to an LSA, and I reminded them that the LSA was a member of college staff. This felt like an important point of clarification as LSAs do not work in schools to be friends with students: they are there to safeguard and to provide academic and wellbeing support. Indeed, one LSA reflected on the importance of discussing boundaries with their students, noting:

> For me, there are some students that will sort of glue on to us because adults tend to be easier to understand than fellow teenagers because you can work out how they work. And that is easier because adults seem to work on a script. Until I became an adult and realised that was a complete lie. I guess my point is that some of the students will glue on to us and one of the things I'm very keen on is to say I'll talk to you. I'm not your friend. I work for the school. I can't be your friend because I'm an adult. We can't have certain discussions because I'm not your friend, but I am someone you can talk to. But I think you have to put down that line. And that was something I was taught at my first school, that you can't be friends with these kids. You can be friendly, but you can't be friends.

Open communication around the LSA's role in upholding school rules and student codes of conduct can also be beneficial in the interests of establishing student–LSA boundaries as it is important for clear expectations around student behaviour to be outlined between LSAs and students from an early point in their work together. Visual reminders are an additional element of boundary reinforcement: it's important that staff lanyards are visible and that LSAs dress in a manner that can clearly distinguish them from students – this is particularly important in my working context, where students are not required to wear uniforms. A good way to establish boundaries in some cases where over-reliance is a concern might also be to rotate LSAs across a variety of lessons, as opposed to assigning LSAs a handful of set students to work closely with over an academic year; this could ensure that students do not depend too closely on a single LSA. Regular check-in with LSA colleagues would be good if you chose to adopt this way of working, to ensure that

The LSA and wellbeing support

your team members are kept in the loop about student progress. It may also be good to review these cases on an individual basis. One LSA I spoke with reflected:

> I also think it's something that should be dealt with in a kind of case-by-case situation because (it may be beneficial) for one student to build a particular rapport with one LSA to support a grounded and solid foundation for that student. But I think it just depends on the needs of the particular student. I think it's definitely a conversation that needs to be had among that team and everyone who's around them and supporting them to ensure that the best approach is taken.

I have also found it important to establish boundaries when it comes to break and lunch times. It can be easy for LSAs and students to eat lunch together, especially if there is a shared learning support centre that they both use. Having lunch together may risk blurring LSA–student social boundaries, however, and it could result in LSAs inadvertently working during their lunch breaks, so I have found it to be good practice for LSAs to have lunch in staff rooms with colleagues. This separation will also be beneficial for students, as it is important for them to have time away from LSAs and for peer groups to have some opportunities to socialise together independently.

> **Top tip:** Do your best to safeguard your break and lunch times and to establish clear non-working boundaries around them. It can be all too easy to chat with students during these times and to start helping them with academic or pastoral matters. This can mean that LSAs risk missing out on their break and lunch times, however, and it's important that you take full advantage of them in order to decompress throughout the day. Once you know that a student is safe, gently tell them that you can check in with them afterwards, and make sure you enjoy your well-earned breaks – eventually, they will come to respect these boundaries and will learn to approach you at a more convenient time.

It can be useful for LSAs to reflect on the boundaries they establish with students as they support them socially. As I outlined in Chapter 1, LSAs can provide students with high levels of socialisation support when it comes to modelling pro-social behaviour in academic support departments. A small number of students may tend to lean on LSAs exclusively for their forms of social connection, however. If you have experienced this, a good rule of thumb is to act as an intentional bridge between these students and their peers. Consider trialling the following strategies:

- Guide and structure student conversations in a manner that intentionally includes those who are more socially reserved – invite them to join in with a peer conversation by posing questions such as 'What do you think?' to boost their involvement.
- Encourage students to join in with peer activities – you might want to encourage them to make a jigsaw together or play a game of Uno or chess in your academic support department.
- Remove yourself from these activities and dialogues incrementally, giving the students space to socialise independently.

> Consider your own work as an LSA here for a moment: how might you support your more socially reserved students to engage with their peers?

Active listening: 'I think the most important thing for the students is to be listened to'

Active listening was identified by numerous LSAs as an integral form of well-being support – one which is perhaps best utilised within safe educational spaces where students feel comfortable to share their thoughts and feelings.

> **Top tip:** Try to make your LSA working space as comfortable and as welcoming as possible for students. Remember that some young people may feel more comfortable chatting when they are engaged in an activity – try to stock up on things like mindful colouring books and pens, as these can be a nice and calming thing for students to engage with. Depending on the layout of your working space, you could also

The LSA and wellbeing support

> organise your academic support rooms to best suit student needs – in my department, for example, we have a low sensory calm space which is specifically for students to access if they are feeling anxious, stressed or overwhelmed.

When reflecting on the importance of active listening, one participant felt: 'My job is to listen... Listen very carefully to the words they use. Take those thoughts and emotions and, if necessary, I can talk to them about it and then record it or I can put a referral to our wellbeing team.' For another LSA, actively listening was particularly important in case they accidentally glazed over a small nuance of what a student had actually said: 'You've got to [really] listen to what they're saying because you might assume they've said something.' Indeed, for a former LSA, a feature of active listening clustered around their ability to consciously lean into a student's frame of reference:

> I listen but you don't just listen with your ears, you kind of listen by reacting: they've got their way of communicating and trying to do something and you've got to sort of go with them on that journey – because you're not going to get them to think and act like you: to get this to work, you have to figure out where they're at and go with them.

Listening without judgement marked a final element of active listing for a different LSA, who noted: 'I think you've just got to have the ears and listen to them and of course not judge.'

> **Top tip:** Be mindful of boundaries when engaging with student wellbeing conversations. It is important that you do not over-share details of your own life when providing support to a student. An LSA highlighted: 'I don't think you should go around and tell everyone. Ohh, well, I do that. I struggle with that.' Taking a detached approach can be a good way to approach these conversations. Another LSA suggested: 'You can talk about things in a kind of detached way about your own life that doesn't give them any details. That helps them understand that you've experienced in a very detached sense similar things.'

Active listening for LSAs is thus detailed and intentional. Its potential to support student wellbeing is perhaps epitomised by a former LSM with seven years of experience in the role, who noted over the course of an interview:

> When teenagers speak, so few people listen to them. But it's about listening to what they have to say and that's as true for supporting wellbeing as it is for somebody who is just struggling to get homework in and Maths. But it's the pinnacle. It's the first thing I used to tell people when they were hired, when they came into the office. Listen: listen at least twice as much as you talk. You are a witness in that space, and they will tell you what help they need from you. For many students over the years, I was their first experience of being listened to. And, actually, for years they've been saying things and people have been patting them on their head or ignoring them and just letting them get on with it. And just the first time that they actually sat down, were allowed to speak and just be heard, the amount of good that could do them was phenomenal.

It may also be a good idea to speak to your line manager about accessing additional training around student wellbeing support if you are interested in developing your pastoral skills as an LSA. One former learning support mentor noted that training in basic counselling and active listening was integral to their work:

> If I was going to pinpoint training that every learning support person should have, it is some kind of very basic counselling skills training. So, I'm not talking about a full qualification or doctorate level or whatnot. When I was in my first year, I signed on for a GCSE-equivalent counselling skills course on how to be a good listener. And it was just little things like mirroring how to be an active listener, how to recognise that most people when they're listening are already thinking about the next question they're going to ask and not actually listening to what's being said. They're more worried about their part in the conversation. I would say that training is something that for the last seven years I used not evenly daily – I used it hourly, if not every 2–3 minutes. And it's something that I still try and use in the classroom and when I'm working with people now.

Little chats and small check-ins

Having small chats with students is another wellbeing support strategy that has worked well for LSAs:

> I would sit with them because sometimes they just need talking to, they just need someone to spend time with them. And I would say to them 'What have you been up to, what's on the agenda for you this week?' And sometimes that's about school, sometimes that's about hobbies. Sometimes that's about what TV show they've been looking at.

Indeed, one LSA noted the value of connecting with students over shared interests:

> You have to get to know them, I think that's what's the most important. Like especially with the school refusers, it's about knowing their favourite movies, then going home and watching them so that you can get on their level. And one of our students is obsessed with a particular film and so now I know pretty much everything about this film so we can talk about it.

For one TSA, it was also important to find the joy in spending time chatting with students as they supported them over the course of their work in academic support:

> Let's not forget to have fun and a bit of humour and be relaxed as well because college is serious enough as it is. There's a lot of pressure to achieve and it's good to have that element of having a bit of banter with your TSA as long as it's within professional boundaries, obviously.

This tip resonates strongly with my experience of working with my students, as the best check-in conversations I have with them often stem from laughing over a joke that someone told or discussing something comical that cropped up in the news. Embrace these moments where you can, as it's important to find joy in the small things when working as an LSA.

Another participant focused on the importance of small details within student check-in conversations as they would chat with students about the things that mattered to them – such as family pets or recent dance competitions – to check in around general student wellbeing: 'It's (remembering) the little things that builds a really positive relationship with those children.' Focusing on these small details is an effective mode of wellbeing support as it communicates an implicit level of care, interest and understanding for students. The LSA is in an optimal position to check in with young people in this manner, as the role is structured in such a way that they will often spend regular blocks of time with students each week as they work with them in lessons. Indeed, as one participant reflected:

> The biggest support for our students is being that consistent face for many of them, so they know that when they go to a particular lesson, there's going to be that consistent face there. The same way of working, the same way of greeting them, and for many of them I find they can come across in a more relaxed way when they know that there's going to be that same face waiting for them and a lot of them really enjoy that.

Top tip: I have often found that it works well to have small walk-and-talk check-ins with my students as we walk to classes together ('How are you doing?' 'How was your morning?' 'How's your day looking this afternoon?'). This approach works quite well for me because often it will give me an insight into how I can best support my student in a lesson. For example, they might say they are feeling tired, so I can then be mindful of encouraging them to take small rest breaks over the course of the lesson should they need to. Small walk-and-talk check-ins are good because they are quite a casual and relaxed way of seeing how a student is doing – some students prefer these types of conversations, as they may feel a bit intimidated or uncomfortable if an LSA were to sit opposite them and ask how they are doing whilst making direct eye contact. Try to check in daily with each student, even if it's just for a two-minute chat as you head to a lesson.

Gentle assertiveness, encouraging rest breaks, providing reassurance and never judging

The LSAs I spoke with reflected on a range of wellbeing support techniques, including:

- Gentle assertiveness
- Rest breaks
- Meditation
- Crafting
- Reassurance
- Record keeping
- Student choice

One TSA considered the value of a **gentle assertiveness** approach to student support, setting clear expectations for their students whilst also remaining mindful of their feelings and preferences: 'Gentle assertiveness is what I call it because there's no point… there's no point being assertive because they won't do it. If you're gentle and kind, they will. But it's a process, isn't it?' The implementation of gentle assertiveness as a strategy was not wholly linear for this TSA; however, this approach encapsulates the importance of striking a balance between supportive understanding and clear educational expectations.

'Time out' strategies can also be used by LSAs to support the wellbeing and emotional regulation of their students, especially those who are younger. One participant noted that they sometimes give their students brain breaks if they show signs of stress: 'Give that child time to kind of regulate their emotions. It might be like having time with a fidget toy or something like that.' Indeed, this strategy reflects the importance of remaining attuned to student emotions and allowing time out for **rest breaks** if they are showing signs of frustration or emotional upset. Try not to draw too much attention to a student needing a rest break if they are feeling overwhelmed in class. I have found that it's better to suggest that they take a break in a calm and casual manner. Rest break cards can also be useful here, as some students can discreetly place them on the table to indicate that they will be taking some time out of their lesson to recalibrate. Remember also to liaise with teachers around student rest breaks, so they are kept in the loop (see Chapter 3 for more details on working with teachers as an LSA).

Meditation was noted as another useful strategy for supporting student wellbeing. One participant mentioned that even 'just two minutes of calming them down could make a difference'. For one LSA, it was important to adopt a holistic and highly empathetic approach to student wellbeing, which recognised that student struggles can come in many different forms. They reflected that some students 'perhaps didn't see their parents as often as they would like to' and that the LSA can hence become 'an important link in the chain' to support students and to listen to them.

There is also evidence to suggest that creative **art and craft** activities can have a positive impact on wellbeing (Keyes et al., 2024; Beltran, 2021). You may want to consider running some creative student enrichment activities, as I have found that its often nice for students to try out different art and craft activities – you could try things like Zentangle, mindful colouring, rock painting, origami or card making. You could also help students to try out crochet or themed collage boards!

> **Top tip:** Try to make the crafting environment as calm and relaxed as possible when you are providing these activities. Make sure the room isn't too crowded and maybe play some ambient music in the background to facilitate a calmer atmosphere.

For some LSAs, it was also incredibly important to provide students with reassurance if they were feeling overwhelmed or upset: '[It's about giving] lots of reassurance and just making sure that they know that they're safe and making sure that they can tell you anything.' Another LSA I spoke with felt it was especially important to **empathise** with students who were upset, and to respect their feelings in such situations:

> Listening is very good and never judging. So they feel how they feel for their own reasons and that's their right. No one should be telling them how they should be feeling or how they should respond to certain situations that may arise in their life. It is their emotions. And the best that you can do is probably listen and give guidance on how to maybe look at a certain situation from a different side. So they'll see a

situation as they see it, but then telling them to come out of that and look in as an outsider in that situation. If it was a friend, for instance, what would they advise their friend and just to have a different perspective on a situation?

One LSA noted that an important aspect of wellbeing support clustered around keeping a **record** of student wellbeing conversations, to ensure they retained a clear record of what was discussed: 'I think record keeping is the single most important part of the job. I always record everything and share information and show evidence of helping and supporting them.' These 'wellbeing notes' do not need to be overly detailed – something like 'Student was upset about X, I signposted them to Y and suggested they do Z' can suffice.

> **Top tip:** It may be a good idea to keep a secure, brief and bullet-pointed record of your wellbeing conversations, and to reflect on them during one-to-one review sessions with a manager. This approach could be helpful in identifying what works well, and it could help to pinpoint areas for future development.

Finally, it can be useful for LSAs to consider factors such as student choice and autonomy when refining their approach to academic and wellbeing support. This may involve working alongside a student to identify individual support strategies that suit their individual needs and preferences.

> **Top tip:** Certain conversation starters can be useful in identifying what will work well for students – for example, asking a student 'If you feel anxious in class, what steps could we take together to help you to feel better? Is there anything I can do to help?' Adopting such a student-focused approach to wellbeing can be useful for LSAs in identifying the solutions that will work best for their students. Make sure you approach these conversations when students are feeling calmer, so they are in an optimal headspace to reflect on what might work well for them moving forward.

LSA motivational strategies: 'Be lavish with praise where it is deserved. Some students with SEND have really difficult lives – positive reinforcement can make a big difference'

Motivation is another important component of the LSA role when it comes to support for student wellbeing, as is helping to build the positive self-concept of young people:

> Students can arrive with a negative experience of the education system, which can colour what they believe that they can achieve in further education. I have always tried to foster a sense of confidence in the students I work with. Students often present with very low levels of self-esteem and it can take some time for an individual to believe that they are capable of success or that they merit the belief that others have in their abilities.

Often LSAs have to encourage their students not only to begin their academic work but to persevere with it when they encounter difficulties. I am often reminded that the current omnipresence of technology can present specific challenges for student learning and wellbeing: distractions can be endless, as young people are often inundated with a never-ending loop of social media content and short-form videos (Lee et al., 2016).

Although motivation is an inherently intrinsic process, LSAs can draw on motivational strategies to inspire their students and to encourage them to engage with their work. I have found that it's useful to adopt a high-energy approach to my academic work with students. On a practical level, this involves taking an organic interest in their work: I actively listen to their ideas, and I try to approach our academic sessions with a positive and well-engaged disposition. I make efforts to intentionally apply this way of working because students are incredibly observant: they can be highly attuned to the attitudes of the people who surround them, and it would be somewhat disingenuous of me to expect enthusiasm and interest from them if I did not convey these attributes myself through things like attentive body language and tone and engaged follow-up questions over the course of our work together. This idea resonated with another LSA I spoke to, who reflected that 'when students see someone who is motivated and eager to help them and get them on the right track, that definitely has the potential to then translate on to them and have a positive impact'.

When motivating students to engage with their work, it is useful to set realistic academic expectations and goals. For example, it may not be feasible for a student with ADHD to sit and work on a written task for an extended period of time, and it is thus useful to tailor expectations and tasks around individual student learning profiles. It can be useful to take small steps when encouraging students to engage with their work and to move away from ideas of an 'all or nothing' approach. One LSA noted this when reflecting on their five-minute approach to working with students: they would give their pupil space to work on a task for five minutes, before checking in on them and praising them for the five minutes of effort that they made. In their words: 'That normally gets them to work for about five minutes or so, but five minutes is five minutes.' For many students, starting can be the most challenging aspect of their studies and five minutes in and of themselves are often worthy of acknowledgement.

In addition to these approaches and strategies, an overarching component of LSA–student motivation concerns the use of praise and positive reinforcement to build pupil self-esteem and self-concept: 'You can do so much. It's hard, it's not easy.' This is particularly important for supporting the wellbeing of students with SEND, many of whom may have previously faced educational challenges and could lack confidence in their academic abilities as a result (Gurney, 1988). It is vital that LSAs celebrate the unique strengths and skills of their students, as is exemplified by one LSA who reflected on the talents of their pupil: 'She's amazing [at LAMDA]. She [dances and reads poetry] beautifully. So, everybody has their talent somewhere.' A large part of meaningful LSA motivation concerns a recognition of student talent and skills. I once knew a student who was highly skilled at print making, for example, and I made sure to compliment the specific details of their print such as its colours and interesting abstract composition, to positively reinforce their view of their artistic abilities.

Strong LSA praise is, in my view, detail orientated as this conveys a genuine level of care and interest that positively contributes to student self-concept. Indeed, in the words of another LSA, 'normally motivation comes down to sort of reminding them like "Hey, you're actually really good at this. I'd like to see what you can do".' Praise and positive reinforcement hence mark useful LSA tools for student motivation and wellbeing. Try to avoid empty and generic praise – focus instead on the small details of a student's work

('Your introduction reads really well; I like how you used clear and concise language there'). Keep in mind also that some students may perceive praise as a demand, or as a form of pressure – in these cases, try to acknowledge what they have done in a less demanding manner, perhaps by indicating your interest and enthusiasm ('This looks interesting; I'd love to know more about how you approach this').

Some key components of motivation can thus include:

- Supporting student self-esteem
- Adopting a high-energy approach to academic working sessions
- Setting realistic goals, chunking tasks and encouraging rest breaks
- Intentional and detail orientated praise

> Consider your own students for a moment. What might some of their individual skills and talents be? What things are they amazing at doing? And how might you draw on these to provide meaningful motivational praise in your educational context?

Nature and wellbeing

A significant body of research supports a positive correlation between nature and wellbeing levels (Martin et al., 2020). Encouraging students to access the natural spaces around them can be useful in supporting their wellbeing – particularly if they are experiencing anxiety or stress (Ewert & Chang, 2018). Humans are innately drawn to the natural world around them (Kellert & Wilson, 1995), and I have found that accessing nature – even by sitting outside on a bench or taking a walk around campus – can help students to regulate their breathing and manage intense emotions during stressful situations. Indeed, the importance of student access to nature was echoed by an LSA who noted that 'we've got tables outside our classrooms so we can sit outside in the fresh air. It's so essential for the children in summer'.

For another LSA, an outdoor walk marked an important component of their wellbeing support for a student:

> There's one student who I've been mentoring and once a week we just go for a walk together around the grounds. Partly because he needs movement breaks and partly because he loves walking and loves

exercise. And also, he just opens up and talks to me on those walks in a way that he wouldn't otherwise. And that enables me then to pick up on some of the things that he's struggling with at school and to perhaps share them with his teachers and that sort of thing.

Access to natural spaces thus has a range of wellbeing benefits, and I have found that it's good to encourage young people to connect with the natural world as much as possible – be that through swimming, hiking, walking or even participating in a Duke of Edinburgh expedition. It can also be beneficial to encourage students to try out different forms of exercise and sport in support of their general health and wellbeing – things such as cheerleading, dancing, table tennis and yoga.

> **Top tip:** Liaise with your line manager and colleagues to see if anyone would like to organise some nature-related wellbeing events in the warmer months. You could run a group nature walk or a litter-picking expedition in the spring/summer terms. Link up with your counselling and wellbeing colleagues to see what you might organise together for your students. You could try something like outdoor yoga or mindfulness sessions.

> Consider your own work as an LSA for a moment. How might you encourage your students to connect with the natural world in support of their health and wellbeing?

Support for LSA wellbeing

From active listening to signposting and student check-ins, LSAs go above and beyond to keep young people safe and well within education. The role is not always easy, however, and it is important that LSAs make time and space to support their own wellbeing to reduce the risk of exhaustion and burnout. Consider the insights below, and reflect on their application to your own working context.

Do not internalise when things go wrong: supporting students academically can be really hard and it's normal for people to have bad days, especially if you are a new starter who is still getting to know a student and their individual needs. Try not to take it personally if your student hasn't achieved a good outcome: the important thing is that you did your best – no good will come from stressing about it and getting burnt out. If things haven't panned out as you hoped, you can always give yourself time and space to refine your working practice: seek advice from SENCOs, specialist teachers or your line manager to identify alternative approaches, training support and strategies for improvement when supporting students with their studies.

Give yourself time and space to learn and develop as an LSA, in full recognition of the challenging and often complex nature of the role. A good tip for refining your practice is to keep a brief and secure log of your student support methods: briefly outline what you did and the effect that it had. Analyse what went well and what didn't, as this will help you to identify future areas for improvement (this can also be good material to review during one-to-ones and probation meetings with your line manager!).

For one former LSM, it was particularly important for LSAs to hold on to the small wins over the course of their work:

> I can add a little bit of advice I would give to learning mentors or LSAs – you've got to enjoy the little things at work. It can become very kind of grinding when you're constantly putting out fires and dealing with bad news or they've not achieved or they've not done quite as well, or they're behind in their homework. As soon as you get that moment of 'Ohh, they did really well in the test, they attended the lesson and they didn't have to go out once'. Yes, brilliant. Hold on to that.

Seek professional support if you are having a difficult time at work. The LSA role can come with unique challenges, and it's normal for LSAs to feel isolated or drained in certain situations. Remember that there is support available, as many educational employers offer counselling and 24-hour wellbeing hotlines that are free and completely confidential.

Actively take breaks throughout your working day. It can be tempting to skip break time to catch up on admin, for example, but taking a 20-minute coffee break is equally important and productive because it will ultimately enable you to return to your work feeling refreshed and mentally recharged. If admin tasks are piling up, speak to your line manager about adding an admin slot to your calendar – it's a good idea to dedicate at least one timetabled period per week to emails and student admin. Don't stress if you cannot get everything done: there are only so many hours in the day, and the reality of working in education is that certain tasks will simply have to be put on the back-burner until you have more time to complete them.

Triage your work tasks throughout the day and try not to feel overwhelmed if you cannot do everything at once. Education is a dynamic and shifting landscape and sometimes unexpected things crop up and take precedence. If a safeguarding concern needs to be logged, for example, take the time to fully focus on it and write it up: you can explain to a teacher why you were late for a class afterwards, in full recognition of the fact that safeguarding was correctly triaged as your top priority.

Lean on your LSA colleagues for support if you need it: share stressful aspects of your work with them and don't hesitate to ask them for advice. A strong team dynamic of mutual support is key to the wellbeing of LSAs, and small acts of kindness – such as offering to cover a lesson for a colleague or making them a cup of tea – can make all the difference in building a compassionate working environment that can help to get someone through a tough day: 'We're very lucky, we can go in our office, have a bit of a rant about it, and if you don't have that, it's just impossible.'

In a similar vein, establish a strong line of communication with your line manager or mentor and do not hesitate to ask for advice and support – especially if you are a new starter. Strong managerial relationships can significantly help LSAs in navigating the daily challenges of their jobs. It's a good idea to get to know your line manager and to find communication patterns that work for both of you. Some line managers have an open door 'drop-in' policy for their team to pop in with questions, but others may prefer that you initially contact them via email to outline what you need help with before dropping by for a chat about it. Establish what works best for you in your own team, and remember that it's good to ask questions.

Consistently assert boundaries throughout your role as an LSA, particularly around break and lunch times. It's a good rule of thumb for LSAs to eat lunch separately from their students if at all possible, as it reinforces the key social boundary that LSAs are members of staff and not peers who eat lunch with students. Having this boundary is really important. If you eat lunch with students, it's likely you will end up focusing on your work and you won't have enjoyed a proper break. Remember that it is also important for students to have time away from LSAs so they can optimally socialise within their independent student friendship groups. Similarly, if you run a club or patrol a yard during lunch, make sure you have time for your own lunch break either before or afterwards.

Asserting these boundaries extends to giving emotional support to students: stay attuned to your own emotions when you are helping a student and remember that it's okay to take a step back if you begin to feel overwhelmed or emotionally drained. In such an instance, make sure the student is physically safe, signpost them to another source of support such as a counsellor or a member of the safeguarding team and take a few minutes for yourself to decompress – accessing nature or a green space within your educational institution can be a good way to recharge after a challenging conversation.

Leave work at work at the end of each day. Do not check work emails outside of your contracted hours: whatever it is can wait until the following day. Try to avoid having the Teams and Outlook apps on your mobile, as it can be all too easy to engage with emails in the evenings if you are getting pop-up notifications on your phone! It's important that you make time to relax and recharge your batteries outside of work: embrace your hobbies as much as possible here, and try to make time in the evening for fun and relaxing activities that you enjoy.

If you are struggling to switch out of work mode after a long and tough day, certain post-work 'rituals' may help you to begin your evening and slowly relax. My post-work ritual begins with changing my clothes: as soon as I come home from work, I change out of my professional work clothes into something more comfortable and relaxing that I associate with being at home. I then usually do my skincare, and I then like to make a beverage to drink as I prepare my evening meal. Each of these steps are small in themselves but they collectively make up a relaxing post-work ritual that enables me to detach from work mode and begin the evening. Things like yoga or exercise can help too! Find out what works for you and embrace it.

Always remember that your wellbeing matters a great deal: a burnt-out LSA will struggle to support their students, so it's very important you take time to look after yourself during term time and holidays.

Concluding reflections

Wellbeing support is, in sum, central to the work of LSAs. 'Unhappy kids don't learn', and it is essential for LSAs to actively contribute to a safe and supportive learning environment for their students. My advice for LSAs would be to draw on your unique educational vantage point to the fullest extent in support of young people: check in with them often, provide motivational support when needed and craft an intentional space for them to openly and safely share any of their worries or concerns. Never forget the importance of your own wellbeing as you engage with this work: look after yourself, take regular breaks, and lean on those around you as you work to support your students over the course of their education.

Consider your own work as an LSA for a moment in light of this chapter. What type of wellbeing support do you provide for your students? Do any of these chapter insights resonate with your working context?

References

Bauld, A. (2021, May 11). Happy Students Are Motivated Students. *Ed. Magazine*. Harvard Graduate School of Education. www.gse.harvard.edu/ideas/ed-magazine/21/05/happy-students-are-motivated-students

Beltran, M. J. (2021). Story: How can art and creativity improve your health and wellbeing? University of the Arts London. www.arts.ac.uk/study-at-ual/short-courses/stories/how-can-art-and-creativity-improve-your-health-and-wellbeing

Cremin, H., & Guilherme, A. (2015). Violence in schools: Perspectives (and hope) from Galtung and Buber. *Educational Philosophy and Theory 48*(11), 1123–1137. https://doi.org/10.1080/00131857.2015.1102038

Dunlop-Bennett, E., Bryant-Tokalau, J., & Dowell, A. (2019). When you ask the fish: Child wellbeing through the eyes of Samoan children. *International Journal of Wellbeing, 9*(4), 97–120. https://doi.org/10.5502/ijw.v9i4.1005

Ewert, A., & Chang, Y. (2018). Levels of nature and stress response. *Behavioural Sciences 8*(5), 49. https://doi.org/10.3390/bs8050049

Firth, J., Gangwisch, J, E., Borisini, A., Wootton, R, E., Mayer, E, A. (2020). Food and mood: How do diet and nutrition affect mental wellbeing? *BMJ 2020* (369), m2382. https://doi.org/10.1136/bmj.m2382

Garvie, D., Pennington, J., Rich, H., & Schofield, M. (2023). Still Living in Limbo: Why the use of temporary accommodation must end. Shelter. https://england.shelter

.org.uk/professional_resources/policy_and_research/policy_library/still_living_in_limbo

Gurney, P. W. (1988). *Self-Esteem in Children with Special Educational Needs*. Routledge.

Hall, S., & Webster, R. (2023). 'It's properly changed, and I think it's going to continue.' How the pandemic and the cost of living crisis remade the teaching assistant role. *Pastoral Care in Education 42*(1), 1–21. https://doi.org/10.1080/02643944.2023.2271483

Kellert, S., & Wilson, E. (1995). *The Biophilia Hypothesis*. Island Press.

Keyes, H., Gradidge, S., Forwood, S. E., Gibson, N., Harvey, A., Kis, E., Mutsatsa, K., Ownsworth, R., Roeloffs, S., & Zawisza, M. (2024). Creating arts and crafting positively predicts subjective wellbeing. *Frontiers in Public Health 12*, 1417997. https://doi.org/10.3389/fpubh.2024.1417997

Lee, A., Son, S-M., & Kim, K. (2016). Information and communication technology overload and social networking service fatigue: A stress perspective. *Computers in Human Behaviour 55*(A), 51–61. https://doi.org/10.1016/j.chb.2015.08.011

Martin, L., White, M., Hunt, A., Richardson, M., Pahl, S., & Burt, J. (2020). Nature contact, nature connectedness and associations with health, wellbeing and pro-environmental behaviours. *Journal of Environmental Psychology 68*, 101389. https://doi.org/10.1016/j.jenvp.2020.101389

McSorley, C., Dunkley, E., & de Ferrer, M. (2023, December 5). High rate of UK teens skipping meals because of poverty, survey suggests. BBC News. www.bbc.co.uk/news/education-67619470

New Economics Foundation. (2012). *Measuring Well-being: A guide for practitioners*. https://neweconomics.org/uploads/files/measuring-wellbeing.pdf

Norwich, B., Moore, D., Stentiford, L., & Hall, D. (2022). A critical consideration of 'mental health and wellbeing' in education: Thinking about school aims in terms of wellbeing. *British Educational Research Journal 48*(4), 803–820. https://doi.org/10.1002/berj.3795

O'Brien, T., & Guiney, D. (2021). Wellbeing: How we make sense of it and what this means for teachers. *Support for Learning 36*(3), 342–355. https://doi.org/10.1111/1467-9604.12366

ONS. (2020). Online bullying in England and Wales: Year ending March 2020. Office for National Statistics. www.ons.gov.uk/peoplepopulationandcommunity/crimeandjustice/bulletins/onlinebullyinginenglandandwales/yearendingmarch2020

Prince's Trust. (2022). *Class of Covid Report 2022*. https://downloads.ctfassets.net/qq0roodynp09/57AtHBpUjehEx5JWXsa5ma/59c709ea468ea6a95e4e71c644f6e40b/Class_of_Covid_Report_2022.pdf

Safeguarding Network. (2024, February). Specific Risks for Children with SEND. https://safeguarding.network/content/safeguarding-resources/specific-risks-children-additional-needs

Trafford, A., Carr M., Ashcroft, D., Chew-Graham, C., Cockcroft, E., Cybulski, L., Garavini, E., Garg, S., Kabir, T., Kapur, N., Temple, R., Webb, R., & Mok, P.

(2023). Temporal trends in eating disorder and self-harm incidence rates among adolescents and young adults in the UK in the 2 years since onset of the COVID-19 pandemic: A population-based study. *The Lancet Child and Adolescent Health 7*(8), 544–554. https://doi.org/10.1016/S2352-4642(23)00126-8

Twenge, J., Haidt, J., Blake, A., McAllister, C., Lemon, H., & Le Roy, A. (2021). Worldwide increases in adolescent loneliness. *Journal of Adolescence 93*(1), 257–269. https://doi.org/10.1016/j.adolescence.2021.06.006

Van Heijst, B. F., Deserno, M. K., Rhebergen, D., & Geurts, H. M. (2020). Autism and depression are connected: A report of two complimentary network studies. *Autism, 24*(3), 680–692. https://doi.org/10.1177/1362361319872373

Wright, N., Hill, J., Sharp, H., & Pickles, A. (2021). Interplay between long-term vulnerability and new risk: Young adolescent and maternal mental health immediately before and during the COVID-19 pandemic. *JCPP Advances 1*(1), e120008. https://doi.org/10.1111/jcv2.12008

3
Strong teacher–LSA working patterns

Chapter outline

Chapter 3 reflects on the architecture of a strong working relationship between teachers and LSAs. I examine:

- The contextual specificity of teacher–LSA working dynamics
- Top tips for LSAs: introductions, outlining working patterns and giving support when needed
- Top tips for teachers: introductions, check-ins and keeping the LSA in the loop
- Strong teacher–LSA communication strategies
- The need for mutual trust and teamwork
- The importance of cultivating camaraderie

Contextual specificity and LSA–teacher working dynamics: 'Often you connect really well with somebody who's been a TA before, they really value you because they've been on the flip side of that [relationship]'

Strong working dynamics between teachers and LSAs are integral to the outcomes of SEND pupils: it is vital that teachers have a clear understanding of the LSA role, and that both parties work well together in class for the benefit of all students (ETF, 2019). Teachers may not always receive training when it comes to the management and direction of support staff, however (Basford et al., 2017), and this gap in the training landscape has been filled as of late with specific resources – such as teacher–TA agreement templates – which clearly outline how TAs can support their teaching colleagues in class (EEF, 2021).

The landscape of LSA–teacher working is marked by its diversity as 'each teacher exists within a specific time, culture and context' (Gidlund, 2018, p.58). Working relationships between LSAs and teachers in the field are very diverse, often shaped by factors such as internal school cultures and the rapport between individual that is established over time: 'Expect a range of relationships with different teachers; not all of them are comfortable with your being there – others will be completely the opposite.' Indeed, one participant I spoke with reflected on the diversity of their work with teachers, noting that their experiences depended largely on individuals:

> It really depends on the teacher, and I think it really depends on their experience. So, some of our teachers here have actually worked as learning coaches or TAs before and you can tell, you can absolutely tell. I feel like partly [this is reflected] in how they use you in quite a positive way, how they talk to you and how they kind of understand the role.

A former LSA noted that their working dynamics with teachers had been largely positive: 'The teachers I worked with have been very receptive. They all really want to help the student' – whilst another LSA reflected on a slightly more mixed experience:

> In some cases – and I'm not saying all because the majority of the teachers that I've worked with have been wonderful and lovely – but with some teachers, there's almost like a pecking order. I think that's a shame because students pick up on that and I think that we are here for a reason and it's a very important reason.

LSAs and teachers thus work together within quite a diverse educational landscape; however, it is important to note that 'the existing literature shows that teachers generally value the contribution that learning support staff make to teaching and learning' (Navarro, 2015, p.38).

> Consider your own work with teachers for a moment. Do you feel you work well together?

Top tips for LSAs: introduce yourself, outline your working patterns, vocalise what you need and establish yourself as a supportive presence

LSA introductions: breaking the ice at the start of the year

Don't hesitate to introduce yourself to your teaching colleagues when you first start working together:

> Drop the tutor an introductory paragraph before you meet them, explaining why you're going to be there and giving an outline of the type of support that you'll be providing. It makes it so much easier for the tutor because (a) they'll get to place a face with a name and (b) there aren't going to be any embarrassing situations where they ask you to do something that's not part of your remit. Because you've already clarified with them exactly what it is that you're going to be doing. So I think, for them, it makes life so much easier being prepared and pre-informed.

This initial introduction can also be useful for teachers, as it can help them to contextualise LSA working patterns, ensuring that both parties are on the same page from an early point in their work together:

> But that's why it's important. I think that we always introduce ourselves beforehand. If I'm with a new student I haven't worked with before, with the teacher I haven't worked with before, I'll go a few minutes before the class, just to introduce myself and to say who I'm there to support. And then we'll have a chat about how they want me to help support them and what is useful when I'm in their classroom to them as a teacher as well. And that's always important. And they are not out of the loop, so to speak.

These early introductions can also help to 'break the ice' between teachers and LSAs, reducing the distance between the two and potentially laying the foundation for a stronger working dynamic to develop over time.

> **Top tip:** I have found that a great way to break the ice with teachers is to talk to them about their subjects – you could talk to a music teacher about a recent concert that you went to, for example!

Outline your working approach and share key information: 'It's about making sure the student and the teachers understand our role'

I have found that it's often worth giving your teaching colleagues a sense of how you will be structuring your support in class at an early point of your working together, so they can factor that into the dynamic of their lessons and accommodate things such as seating plans etc (e.g. 'I'll be taking some notes at the back and floating across the room to provide check-in support with tasks'). This approach is often useful for teachers, as it can help to contextualise LSA working approaches, ensuring that both parties are on the same page from an early point in their work together. Indeed, as one TSA I spoke to noted:

> It's about making sure the student and the teachers understand our role. It's very important they understand why we're in a classroom. What are we doing? Even the most experienced teachers, who are very much in charge of their classroom and have lots of experience, sometimes do not always understand our role. And I think it's very important to remind them what you're there for, who you're here for and so on. Update them on the progress of your students and find out initially what the work is about. They should be directing you, it should be very close collaborative work.

Teachers can also welcome the input of LSAs, particularly when it comes to sharing key information regarding student support and what might work best in the classroom:

> It's very hard to hold information in your head about more than 20 students and then the other classes that you teach. Whereas the LSA

may have more familiarity with those individuals in that classroom, so when they can input that information, it's helpful.

Indeed, another teacher noted that it was useful for LSAs to 'feedback about what is working for the student and what is not working, so the teacher can adapt and differentiate to meet the students' needs more'.

> **Top tip:** Don't be shy to share your student support ideas with teachers. It's also a good idea to let them know if your approach to student support changes or if you are trialling a new method in class – drop them a quick email to let them know what you are doing. Try to communicate with them ahead of time if possible, to ensure they are informed of key changes in advance – for example, 'I am trialling a check-in form of support this week. Please don't hesitate to get in touch if you need anything from me or if you have any questions.'

Get involved where it's appropriate: 'You can't be a wallflower as a TSA'

For one teacher I spoke to, it was beneficial for LSAs to actively get involved in their lessons:

> I think sometimes the support for an individual student makes the LSA a bit invisible to the rest of the class, and actually it's much better to have visibility. So I really like an LSA who is kind of observant enough to respond to the group dynamic which can change, and if somebody needs a nudge to refocus, that's helpful. It's [about] everybody kind of working for the same sort of end, I think. So that's really nice when that happens.

Indeed, another teacher noted that it was always worth it for LSAs to get stuck into their lessons:

It would be helpful for LSAs to move around the room, interacting with all students, reminding, coaching, guiding, supporting. It's really nice for a teacher to have the support too – I'd say feel free to get involved to the max if you and the teacher agree you're comfortable and this is appropriate.

I have definitely found that it is worth getting involved in lessons in this way as an LSA, particularly when it comes to subjects that I am quite familiar with. It is often rewarding to work across classes with a range of students, and my own students with EHCPs often prefer me to structure my support in this way as it takes the sole focus away from them during their lessons.

Another good way to get involved as an LSA is to contribute to in-class discussions, under the right circumstances. Try to find organic ways of facilitating this – there may be a natural pause during a lesson and you could use that moment to vocalise an idea. The timings of these contributions are key; one teacher I spoke to noted:

> I do like [LSA contributions] as long as it's well timed. When I'm whole-class teaching, if the other adults in the room can think of other examples or relate it to other experiences, I find that helps. I don't mind those interjections at all as long as they are appropriately timed.

Your role in this way could be that of a sounding board, as I have often found it useful to vocalise some initial brainstorming ideas to help break the dialogic ice during lessons. It's often good to read the room with respect to these contributions, as one LSA noted that they 'participate in the lesson where it works. On one or two occasions, very tentatively, I have even offered my own thought as a contribution to a discussion. And again, you have to know your teacher to know whether that is welcome or not.'

Top tip: Be mindful not to over-contribute when participating in class-based discussions, I had a tendency to do this at an early stage in my practice as an LSA, especially if I was very interested in a particular topic that was being discussed in class! Try to avoid this when working as an LSA: there is an art to getting in-class contributions right, and a good rule of thumb is to lean into natural pauses and to fill them as and when they arise. Some teachers may even appreciate your input in this respect, especially if your contribution is relevant and well thought-out!

Consider your own work as an LSA for a moment. How might you become more involved in the classes that you attend? What might an optimal level of involvement look like in your working context?

Establish yourself as a supportive presence: avoiding corrections, remaining engaged and offering to help out if needed

When working as an LSA alongside your teaching colleagues, try to establish yourself as a **supportive presence** in the room. The classroom is the domain of the teacher, and it's understandable that they may feel observed or under pressure if another adult is present who could alter the dynamic of their teaching space:

> I think sometimes the teacher can feel quite overwhelmed as well; sometimes I think [they] can find it difficult and intimidating to have the LSA in the room because it is a particular vantage point. I can understand why they feel like they have adults watching them in their space.

This idea of feeling observed by an LSA was echoed by a teacher I spoke with, who reflected:

> Say [the LSA] looks bored or he looks judgemental. That makes me feel very uncomfortable because it's very exposing to be leading a lesson. And if somebody is giving the signals that they're disinterested,

that you're being boring, it's hard to keep teaching because you think if the adult can't sit through this, then probably the students can't as well. So that's quite frustrating.

It thus becomes important, in my view, to communicate your interest as an LSA: show your teaching colleagues that you are following the thread of their lesson and that you are engaging with what they are saying.

Indeed, this was especially important for one teacher, who noted the challenges of working alongside 'a **disengaged** LSA who is sitting in the classroom not doing much, on their phone so not engaging with the student and classwork. Looking bored and having no idea of what is being taught and not caring.' Adopting a positive and professional way of being in a classroom is additionally very important throughout the course of your work with your students, who may look to you as a positive role model. They are likely to mirror the body language and the actions of the people around them, and this adds to the importance of adopting a positive and engaged outlook when attending lessons as an LSA.

> **Top tip:** I appreciate that it can be challenging and quite mentally exhausting to engage academically all day, especially if you have a full schedule of lessons as an LSA. Make the most of your break and lunch times to mentally recalibrate, and you can always take a five-minute rest break yourself if you need a drink of water or some fresh air to help you to regain your focus during lessons. Try to weave in natural movement breaks as well – for example, by going to print a document if you need it during a lesson.

In the interests of supporting your teaching colleagues, make sure to avoid things such as in-class **corrections**, as they have the potential to make teachers feel uncomfortable and on-the-spot in class:

> We have to be careful not to step on their toes... I remember one LSA who picked up a wrong spelling of the teacher and I think later on she was told by the teacher not to do it in front of the class.

Be careful also not to interrupt your teaching colleagues. One teacher I spoke to advised LSAs to '[avoid] interrupting the teacher mid conversation – when the teacher is teaching, giving instructions or giving feedback. This causes confusion for students as they are trying to listen to two people.' It's quite a good rule of thumb to be mindful of noise levels generally when working in lessons with teachers: it's fine to check in with your students as you scaffold tasks, for example, but try to do so in a more hushed tone so as not to disrupt the focus of others in the room. You can also always have a chat with a teacher at the end of a lesson, if there is something you need to update them with.

I also think it's good practice to attend classes **punctually**, as this will set a positive example for students: message your teaching colleague if you are running late and keep them in the loop as to why (e.g. a student is having a tough morning and may need extra time to make it to the classroom). Small details like this can show an extra layer of consideration, as it could be slightly off-putting for a teacher if an LSA walked into their classroom late without having provided any context as to why.

Be attentive to wider class dynamics as an LSA and use your unique vantage point to support your teaching colleagues: 'I think because you're on the ground all the time in the classroom, you see things that other people don't see.' Keep tabs on how other groups are progressing with their work and offer your assistance once you have established that your primary (EHCP) student is able to approach a chunk of their task independently. In this way, you can provide support by acting as a **second pair of eyes** in the classroom:

> This might be more relevant with lower school kids when they're doing activity-based work and [the LSA] can go around and say, 'I've spotted there's a group over there that either aren't focused or are a bit behind or struggling with something.' It doesn't even have to be the student you're dealing with [who has the EHCP]; obviously, they're your prime concern, but in the right circumstances, that might kind of build trust.

I also think it's useful for LSAs to reflect on the extent to which teaching can be a highly demanding profession. Teachers often grapple with high workloads and elevated levels of stress (National Education Union, 2024), and it is in the midst of this working context that a **helping hand** from an LSA may provide a glimmer of useful support. Let your teaching colleagues know that you are there to help, and be willing to lend a hand if needed: 'We have gained a good reputation and more trust from teachers at college. So they know they can rely on us and they really appreciate what we do with the students.'

Always ask if you are not sure

It's important to always ask for help and guidance if you are not sure about something as an LSA. Teachers will have access to a plethora of resources, help sheets, revision guides and example essays, and they will likely be willing to share them with you and have a chat if you require further information. Teachers, moreover, will not expect you to be a subject expert and it's completely reasonable to reach out if you need to for some guidance. Questions, as a rule of thumb, are very good – they show good interest and a willingness to learn. Don't hesitate to reach out to gather the information that you need to support your students.

Remember that consistency is key

Finally, consistency around teacher–LSA partnerships can be quite helpful in building up a rapport and establishing strong working patterns over time. Try to work consistently with your teaching colleagues if at all possible, as it's worth spending the extra time with them to familiarise yourself with their teaching styles and the manner in which you can best support them in class:

> One thing I find sort of frustrating is that I don't work with the same student consistently across the subject. So, I think the most I have is four out of six lessons with any particular class, so you never really get to feel you have that close relationship with the class teacher.

Be mindful as well of not confusing students by suggesting methods that differ from those of the class teacher. Consistent teaching is very important, and LSAs may inadvertently cause confusion by suggesting that students trial different methods to those that are taught in class. In my experience, this is more likely to happen in subjects such as Maths, as there are a variety of methods that people can draw on to structure their answers for particular topics. Indeed, one teacher suggested:

LSAs could check with teachers if alternative methods are being taught by the LSA to the student, to ensure that the methods are approved and used in the curriculum. It would be in the interest of both the LSA and the teacher that they know what the student is learning and can tailor the teaching methods to suit the student.

LSAs can thus trial a range of approaches in order to cultivate strong partnerships with their teaching colleagues, including:

- Breaking the ice at the start of the year
- Outlining key working patterns
- Boosting in-class involvement
- Avoiding corrections, remaining engaged and offering to help out
- Seeking guidance if needed
- Working consistently with teaching colleagues

> Consider your own work with teachers for a moment. What strategies might you employ to strengthen your working dynamics in class?

Top tips for teachers: introductions, check-ins and keeping LSAs in the loop

Teachers can also consider a range of small but effective steps to strengthen their working relationships with LSAs.

Small things such as a quick **greeting** can go a long way in making your LSAs feel valued and welcome in the classroom. This was particularly important for one LSA, who reflected:

> [Students] need to see that we have a good relationship with the teacher. They feel it, they see it if you say hello and how are you to the teacher. They will feel like, oh, they have [a good working dynamic]. It's very important to have a good relationship with them.

If you can, try to carve out a few extra minutes to **get to know** the LSAs you work with: take five minutes to chat with them, and to learn about their aspirations and academic backgrounds. This small chat could even yield some useful in-class support strategies. You could discover, for example, that the LSA has a degree in your subject and is well placed to work alongside you in class to offer guidance and support to students. One teacher I spoke with reflected on their strong working partnership with a support staff colleague, noting: 'I think my partnership with my colleague has been really successful and because that colleague has a background in modern foreign languages and EAL teaching, I think those sort of skill sets are very complementary for our GCSE resit.'

Introduce new LSAs to your class: 'I think the best teachers, if they have got a new LSA in the room, they'll introduce them at the start.' (It is often worth clarifying who the LSA is and what their position is in the classroom. An LSA I spoke to was once mistaken for an inspector when a student asked them, 'What are you doing here, Sir? Are you inspecting the teacher?'!)

Try to avoid **'call-out' questions** such as asking an LSA 'Who are you here to support?' in front of a class, as this can potentially be embarrassing for the student in question who might wish to keep a low profile. Consider utilising another method of accessing this information, such as checking a SEND register or chatting to an LSA at the side of the class. You can also always ping the LSA a message via Teams!

Make a space for LSAs to sit in class and provide them with **access to key learning materials.** This might mean adding them to a subject Teams channel or photocopying an extra worksheet to ensure there is one for them to use in class. It is a good idea to provide LSAs with resources such as answer booklets or formula sheets – especially in subjects such as Maths – so they can easily look up answers and follow the thread of a lesson in support of their student.

Consider instructions around **noise levels**. It is completely understandable for teachers to call for silent working in class, but LSAs may also need to have muted dialogue with their students to check their task progression and to provide further support. One LSA I spoke to noted that this was a particular challenge for their colleague on one occasion, as a student had asked them a question in class about some emotional regulation cards and they were asked to leave the room by a teacher: 'They felt mortified because they were talking with the student that they were there for and the teacher asked them to step outside and have the conversation with the student outside.'

> **Top tip:** Tweak calls for silence in class by adding the phrase 'unless you are talking to a member of staff', as this small alteration can help LSAs with their in-class support.

Keep LSAs in the loop where possible. If you craft weekly **lesson plans or use key schemes of work**, for example, consider sharing them with your LSA so they are aware of upcoming topics and deadlines in class:

> It's helpful if you're working regularly with the teacher, if they keep you informed about what is coming up in terms of the curriculum so it's not a surprise. It's great if the teacher can prepare you for what's coming up so you can read ahead if you've got time, but even if you don't actually look at the materials, at least you know what's happening and what journey that students on.

Don't hesitate to **ask for LSA input and support**, especially if you are trying to ascertain what might work best for a particular student. LSAs work closely with their students and are often aware of the specific support strategies that can work well for each one; they can thus often give teachers useful feedback about certain in-class tweaks that could benefit their students. This worked well in practice for one LSA I spoke to, who reflected:

> If we [as LSAs] can draw their attention to small tweaks that we know from getting to know those students, [we can highlight] the little things that will help them to include the experience for those people. I think we have quite a big role to play in that. And teachers who welcome that or even ask for it, that's really good. It could even be little things, like those students who need movement breaks. It's such an easy thing to do to [say] to a teacher when you need some books handed out, please ask so-and-so to do it and they get out of their chair and wander around. It's the sort of thing they might not think about, and they'll be only very happy to have an LSA advocating in that way.

Try, where possible, to include both the student and the LSA in **feedback and learning conversations**. There are a range of ways you may want to structure this, but I have found it useful in the past to take notes whilst teachers communicate feedback to students, for example. This area was particularly important for one LSA, who reflected on the idea of a **triad working structure** between teachers, LSAs and students:

> There should be a triad relationship between teacher and student where the teachers have got this specialist knowledge and they have to make sure that it comes across to the student, and we as LSAs sort of bridge that gap between the two.

The LSA will ideally act as a bridge between students and teachers, encouraging them to access in-class information and help in a manner that is optimal for them. Indeed, one LSA noted:

> I think that goes back to dialogue and to the importance of establishing a kind of ethos of collaboration and empathy. I think there are a number of ways that you can do that in terms of putting it in the students' hands to communicate their availability, putting it in their hands to communicate the specific areas of support that they feel they need and the little things that you can do to show that kind of respect.

Embrace **adaptive teaching** where you can and check in with your LSAs about what may need to be adapted to support their students – you can always work alongside an LSA to develop specific resources if you feel that would be helpful.

Avoid **reprimanding** an LSA in front of their student, or an entire class, as doing so undermines the professional standing of LSAs and risks straining working relationships. If there is an issue you would like to address with an LSA, consider discussing it outside the classroom or at the end of the lesson: 'If there was a problem with the LSA, then speak to the LSA after class rather than in front of students.'

Teachers can thus cultivate strong working relationships with LSAs by:

- Getting to know the LSA
- Avoiding call-out questions
- Ensuring the LSA has access to key materials
- Tempering instructions around noise levels
- Sharing resources and lesson plans

- Welcoming LSA input and feedback
- Adopting a triad of communication between teacher, LSA and student
- Avoiding reprimands in class

> Consider your own work with the LSAs in your class for a moment. How might you strengthen your working dynamic moving forwards?

Strong teacher–LSA communication: clear instructions, corridor chats, Teams check-ins and reading the room

Good communication between teachers and LSAs can significantly enhance the learning experiences of SEND students as it supports clarity of purpose and joined-up thinking:

> I think the best way for teachers and LSAs to work together is just having that communication. So [it's about] not being afraid to speak to the teacher to ask for a bit more direction or maybe their input. I think it really improves my support for a student when I talk to the teacher, because then you can talk about what they're going to do in the lesson or what they're going to do in future work and things like that. So one of the ways that I found was really helpful for the one-to-one study sessions, there was one student who was [a bit stuck] and the teacher really wanted to help and we would [communicate] outside of the lessons and via email as well, just to talk about how best to approach things. And then she would also send me worksheets, just to go through everything. So I think it's just best to have open communication between teachers and LSAs.

Checking in with a teacher over the course of a lesson is a key aspect of the teacher–LSA working relationship, as it can enable key student progress updates to be exchanged over the course of the day. Often it can be good to structure these check-ins at the beginning and end of each lesson: 'It's just keeping up to date with each other and just having that little one- or **two-minute conversation** at the beginning and at the end. It does so much. It does so much for such a little amount of time.' Often this can be a good opportunity to touch base on how certain students are doing, to ensure both the teacher and the LSA remain on the same page regarding student progress:

'At the end of the lesson, normally when all the students are gone, we have that moment to say, Oh, so-and-so seemed a bit off today, and they go, Oh yeah, I don't know what's going on with that.'

This two-minute catch-up is small in itself, yet it can go very far in enabling LSAs to feel that they are working well with their teaching colleagues:

> When teachers say 'If you're not sure, I've got an answer sheet if you need to have a look at the answers and see if people are doing it right', that, to me, is what a strong working relationship is like: it's that teamwork and it should be a team thing because we're both there to improve a student's learning, and being able to have that little conversation at the start and at the end to say 'Here are some details, here are some people I want you to work with', it goes a long way, it really does.

This was supported by one teacher who contributed to this book, who highlighted the importance of checking in with LSAs in real time: 'Talk in person, in class. In my experience, all efforts to collaborate ahead of time just sadly aren't practical.'

> **Top tip:** Be mindful of teachers' time when checking in, as they often can be very busy over the course of the academic year. Try to be flexible when checking in, and consider catching up at a different time if that would be more convenient for them. It's also a good idea for LSAs to attend department meetings with their teaching colleagues, as this could be a good space to keep them in the loop when it comes to things such as lesson plans and upcoming assessments.

For one TSA I spoke with, strong communication was characterised by 'consistency, speed, accuracy, relevance and the sharing of important information'. **Clear instructions** from teachers can also work well for LSAs in class: 'The last teacher that I worked with, we had an amazing working relationship. I knew exactly where she wanted me to be every second of the day because she gave me very good direction.' Indeed, another LSA noted that strong communication was 'really clear-cut right at the start of the lesson:

here's the expectation, here's what I want you to do'. On a practical level, one LSA welcomed quite an instrumental and direct approach from teachers when it came to their in-class communication: 'The teachers would pinpoint me, we're going to do this: I want you to find questions on this, and that's how we worked and it's wonderful when you see the results.'

Other LSAs also noted that communication via **Teams** and email enabled them to catch up with teachers and exchange views on student progress and support:

> I've got quite a good relationship with quite a few teachers. It's obviously talking to them if you can, just before the lesson and after the lesson; also talking on Teams seems to work really well. Obviously, a lot of them you don't see for a couple of days, and you can exchange updates via Teams.

I have found that Teams communications can be a good way to check in with teachers, particularly if I have any follow-up questions that I may not have had time to ask at the end of the lesson. This was also true for a teacher I spoke with, who noted: 'Knowing that colleagues are responsive to Teams messaging or emails, to know that those channels are used and accessed, I think it's quite helpful.'

In addition to Teams and email communication, corridor conversations can enable teachers and LSAs to exchange useful information in a more casual manner. For one former LSM, an important aspect of good communication clustered around being **visible** and known to their colleagues:

> I need to be visible and known to the teachers. But also people would stop me in the corridor and say, 'Oh, X student is a bit behind on homework. Next time you see her next week, can you just see what's going on with that?' That's a corridor conversation. That's not an email that's been sent, that they've got to find time to send to me. That's not me dropping by their office. That's they've seen me often enough and I've dropped by their office and said I'm working with X and we're aware of this. This is often a strategy going forward. That teacher then knows what I look like, knows what my name is in the corridor that they can go, Oh, just on your way past, just so you're aware...' That kind of openness, that awareness can really help teachers.

Finally, strong communication between teachers and LSAs requires a high level of attention. It is important for LSAs to 'read the room', to attune themselves to the core thread of a lesson and pick up on subtle signals from the teacher that their input might be welcome. Good communication, in many ways, clusters around a strong reading of body language. One teacher I spoke to reflected:

> That's why relationship building is important because with somebody like my colleague, when she's supporting, I can signal that I need another example – quick, can you think? When you've worked with somebody a long time, they're sort of attuned to your signals, aren't they? And they are quite subtle signals; it's not even a beckon, **it's a glance**. It's an exchange of looks of one person to another person who knows 'yeah, I need to chip in'.

Teachers and LSAs can thus trial a range of communication strategies, including:

- Class check-ins
- Direct, clear-cut instructions
- Teams and email communications
- Corridor catch-ups
- Tuning in to teacher signals

> Consider your own work with teachers for a moment. What might optimal communication look like in your working context?

Reciprocal feedback, learning from LSAs and working collaboratively as a team: 'There's got to be some mutual trust and respect'

In addition to good communication, **mutual trust and respect** are integral to positive teacher–LSA working relationships: 'There's got to be some mutual trust and respect.' Often it can be good in practice for teachers to check in with LSAs and to consider the value of their educational perspective. This can work especially well when it comes to lesson delivery and impact. One LSA noted:

> We're often sat with the children so we get the view of the lesson delivery that they get as well. So, if you have a child with working memory/processing issues, you could say, hang on, those instructions were too fast. [The teacher may not have picked up on this] because they're standing at the front delivering.

It could also be beneficial for teachers to embrace the SEND knowledge base of LSAs, factoring in their ideas when it comes to student support and anticipating certain in-class issues:

> You're here supporting these students. What can you tell me about them? Can you let me know if you're aware of something that might be coming up before the lesson? Can you let me know if it's been a bad day for them or give me that warning? Because if you can give me that warning now, I'm not going to turn around to them halfway through a lesson, and ask them a question that they refuse to answer because they're not in the headspace for it.

Working dynamics between teachers and LSAs can thus benefit from a process of **reciprocal feedback** whereby teachers can 'trust the LSA and maybe take insight from the LSA as well'. Indeed, the value of inclusive and reciprocal feedback was summed up by one LSA, who reflected on the essence of a strong teacher–LSA relationship and noted:

> The word that came to mind was inclusivity and that's in the planning, the feedback, like across the board, you have to be inclusive of each other as well. It works both ways. Reciprocal feedback, I think that doesn't happen a lot. I think it tends to be one way.

Within this frame of mutual trust and respect, it is useful to view the LSA as an **educational collaborator** and a fellow member of the team:

> We all have our role to play absolutely, but from the students' point of view, I do think we need to be united. Certainly we've got [some separation] and this is my role and they are the subject specialists, but

from the students' point of view, we need to be a united front, **we are a team**.

This was echoed by a teacher, who noted that there should be 'equality in the workplace to ensure respect – we are all there to support and guide students to achieve'.

When reflecting on their roles, many LSAs also highlighted the importance of **actively supporting** the teachers they worked with in class: 'I think that often our jobs are to support the teachers; support is needed sometimes because teachers nowadays have a huge workload.' It can thus be useful for teachers to view the LSA as a member of their team and a fellow adult in the room who is available to provide assistance. Many LSAs recognise how busy teachers are and are very keen to provide assistance where possible: 'We're there to help.'

Remembering small details and cultivating camaraderie: 'I think it's so important to actually get to know the tutor as a person'

Finally, for many LSAs, a foundational element of their strong working relationships with teachers stemmed from the time that they spent together when they got to know each other as people. From having a quick chat and a laugh together in class, to remembering small details such as birthdays, strong teacher–LSA relationships are built over time through seemingly small interactions that collectively culminated in an overarching sense of camaraderie and **goodwill.** Indeed, one LSA noted:

> I think it's so important to actually get to know the tutor as a person as well. I think you put a better impression on them if you just ask them how they are, how's your day been. You know, [ask them] what have you been up to, because then if you're with them all the time, they get used to you and then they kind of want to be back with you rather than have someone else that's in their space, in their class.

For one HLTA, remembering small things went a long way in building a strong working dynamic with teaching colleagues: 'I just think little things like remembering when your teacher's birthday is and all of those [small] things go towards having a nice working relationship, they really make a big difference.' Another LSA noted that **laughter** was an important component of their work with teachers in class as it helped to produce a joyful and harmonious working environment whereby both parties felt happy and at ease with one another:

> I think you've got to remember to laugh. I think you need non-confrontational behaviours to be in place because I think whether that's to your LSA or whether that's to the child, it hugely impacts how you can maintain the relationship between the three of you.

Cultivating an awareness of how to build relationships with people can also be hugely helpful in this area. One LSA highlighted the importance of enhancing **soft skills** when working with teachers and indeed in education generally:

> A lot of it is just about the kinds of people that people are. And it's actually having the soft skills to know how to work with people, whether it's the students, whether it's other teachers who even work with yourself and also in terms of your own presentation. But having that awareness and those kinds of skills to be natural but to be able to read situations and to communicate with people, that's what you have to do to work in education.

Strong teacher–LSA working dynamics thus stem from the process of building a relationship in and of itself, and it is fundamentally worth taking the time to chat and to get to know one another as colleagues and as people (whilst taking appropriate professional boundaries into account, of course!). Indeed, for one LSA, working with the same teacher and getting to know them over an extended period of time culminated in an enjoyable in-class dynamic of **camaraderie**:

> The social aspect between an LSA and a teacher is if you're with a student that started for the first time in a subject and they have that same teacher the next year, you [and the teacher] can just bounce off each other perfectly. I think that's one of the most satisfying moments.

Concluding reflections

Strong teacher–LSA working relationships are not born overnight. Many develop over time, nurtured by small acts of goodwill and an overarching respect for the other as an educator. Good teacher–LSA relationships are shaped by strong understandings, a mutual sense of teamwork and an effective system of communication that works for both parties. Whilst individual dynamics will undoubtedly differ in practice, this chapter has explored some core elements of the teacher–LSA relationship that have worked well for practitioners in the field. I would encourage LSAs and teachers reading this to remember that you are, at the end of the day, united in the common goal of providing support for students – embrace the spirit of collaboration as you move forward together to better the lives of young people.

> Consider your own working relationships with LSAs and teachers for a moment. How might you adapt some of these key chapter ideas to suit your working context? What might a strong teacher–LSA relationship look like for you personally, and what steps might you take in order to bring it to fruition?

References

Basford, E., Butt, G., & Newton, R. (2017). To what extent are teaching assistants *really* managed?: 'I was thrown in the deep end, really; I just had to more or less get on with it.' *School Leadership & Management* 37(3), 288–310. https://doi.org/10.1080/13632434.2017.1324842

Education Endowment Foundation (EEF). (2021). *Making Best Use of Teaching Assistants: Guidance Report*. https://educationendowmentfoundation.org.uk/education-evidence/guidance-reports/teaching-assistants

Education & Training Foundation (ETF). (2019). *Learning Support Assistants in Further Education and Training: Guidance for Leaders and Managers*. www.et-foundation.co.uk/document/learning-support-assistants-in-further-education-and-training-guidance-for-leaders-and-managers

Gidlund, U. (2018). Teachers' attitudes towards including students with emotional and behavioural difficulties in mainstream school: A systematic research synthesis. *International Journal of Learning Teaching and Educational Research* 17(2), 45–63. https://doi.org/10.26803/ijlter.17.2.3

National Education Union. (2024, April 3). State of education: workload and wellbeing: the majority of teachers are struggling with workload. https://neu.org.uk/latest/press-releases/state-education-workload-and-wellbeing

Navarro, M. F. (2015). Learning support staff: A literature review. OECD Education Working Paper No. 125. https://doi.org/10.1787/5jrnzm39w45l-en.

4
Responding to challenging behaviour as an LSA

Chapter outline

Chapter 4 considers a range of challenging behaviours that LSAs may encounter over the course of their work in academic support. I examine a range of solution-focused strategies, as I reflect on:

- The role of the LSA in responding to challenging behaviour
- Contextualising student behaviour
- Identifying triggers
- Remaining calm and embracing de-escalation tactics
- Working with teachers to manage behaviour
- Navigating rejection as an LSA
- Supporting reluctant workers to engage
- Mediative and restorative approaches to challenging behaviour
- Behaviour management in primary contexts

The role of the LSA in responding to challenging behaviour

LSAs will commonly encounter a range of challenging behaviours over the course of their work in academic support. Challenging behaviour is a broad concept, and it is often used to refer to forms of behaviour that can challenge or impede learning (Aas et al., 2023). The specificities of such behaviour will largely depend on individual contexts but some core examples might include request opposition, high noise levels, a lack of respect for others and their space, aggression towards peers or destruction of property (Guikas & Morin,

DOI: 10.4324/9781003480648-5

2021, p.1157). LSAs may also encounter issues such as emotional dysregulation, rudeness, profanity, tantrums, work refusal or class avoidance. Students can also present with forms of challenging behaviour that occur in more of a relational context, impacting their relationships with teachers and peers. Responding to challenging behaviour is key to the work of LSAs, who are, in many ways, the frontline workers on the ground who will need to respond to their students in moments of unhappiness and distress. I have personally found that responses to this type of behaviour must be very carefully crafted, as it is crucial for LSAs to maintain strong working relationships with their students. I engage with these considerations in detail in this chapter, as I provide some tips for LSAs who are interested in reflecting on this area of their practice.

> Consider your own work as an LSA for a moment. How have you navigated behavioural challenges in the past? What do you think the role of the LSA should be when it comes to responding to challenging behaviour?

Contextualising student behaviour

When responding to challenging behaviour as an LSA, a good rule of thumb centres around questions of context: it is important to consider why a student may be presenting with certain behaviours, so you can begin to craft an appropriate response. This was highlighted by one LSA I spoke with, who noted:

> When I encounter [challenging behaviour], I try to understand the underlying causes of the behaviour. For example, ADHD or autism or oppositional defiance disorders. Last year I had a student with a [specific] sensory profile and he really couldn't cope with noise, even with someone sniffing. He couldn't cope with it, so he always had noise-cancelling headphones and [it was important to know] what would disturb his focus in the lesson so I could examine and assess what would work for him.

> **Top tip:** Remember that not all students will be aware of what constitutes an appropriate standard of behaviour in educational settings and it is important for those in academic support roles, such as LSAs, to make these expectations clear by actively modelling and reinforcing pro-social behaviours. You are not alone in responding to challenging student behaviour: always liaise with a SENCO or manager if a student is presenting with behaviour that you are struggling with, as you can request further guidance and training if you feel you would benefit. I also think there is value in cultivating a compassionate view of challenging behaviour where possible. Try to hold space for the emotions and experiences of young people, as many who exhibit challenging behaviours may experience social difficulties over the course of their lives, and it is important they are surrounded by supportive and understanding professionals in education who are equipped to meet their needs. Finally, keep in mind the importance of accurate language when discussing student behaviour, in the interests of holistic understanding (e.g. by acknowledging that a student is demand avoidant as opposed to 'stubborn').

In some cases, it can also be good to initiate dialogue with students around certain behaviours and responses. For example, if a student has refused to attend their lesson, it may be useful to have a chat with them to examine the situation in more detail – they may be unwilling to attend due to a serious issue such as bullying, or it could be the case that they are anxious about a seating arrangement or worried about being publicly called on to contribute to a discussion in class. Once this information has been shared and discussed, you can provide solution-focused reassurance – for example, by offering to check in with the class teacher, and to ask the teacher not to openly call on the student to answer questions in class.

Try to adopt a solution-focused approach to these situations: let the student know that you are there to support them, and that you will advocate for a solution that will best suit their needs. Keep in mind also that a core element of your role is to encourage your students to attend their lessons if at all possible: the LSA is not a qualified teacher, and students risk missing out on vital specialist instruction if they opt to complete work alongside their LSAs in academic support departments (Breyer et al., 2021). The primary goal should thus always be for them to attend. Try to think outside the box if they are having difficulties in this area, so you can brainstorm alternative solutions – might they be willing to dial into a lesson via Teams from an academic support department, for example? Consider what might work for your students, in order to support them in accessing their learning.

> Consider your own work as an LSA here for a moment. What forms of challenging behaviour have you previously encountered?

Identifying student triggers and stress points: remaining attuned to student mannerisms and their individual ways of expressing themselves

In addition to questions of context, it is also important to consider individual triggers and stress points when responding to challenges of behaviour. Be observant as you work with your students: take note of how they respond to certain situations and try to identify what may be triggering certain responses. A student may, for example, be very unwilling to attend a lesson because of sensory sensitivities around loud noises or feelings of claustrophobia in a classroom. In this instance, you could work with them to identify solutions, such as providing them with noise-cancelling headphones or helping them to secure a seat nearest the classroom door so they could easily access an exit should they need it. Change can also be a source of stress for some autistic students (National Autistic Society, 2020), and a large part of LSA support in that context may be around providing as much advance notice as possible if a change to their routine is imminent. Whilst there is no one-size-fits-all approach to supporting students, it is useful to consider their specific triggers and to formulate solutions that address them to as large an extent as possible: 'There's definitely something to be said for understanding a student's triggers or [the] factors that might be playing a role in the behaviour.'

> **Top tip:** Keep an eye out for signs which may indicate that a student is on the verge of becoming very stressed or upset in class. These will vary based on individual students, but they can sometimes include signs such as irritability, fidgeting with objects around them or difficulty concentrating (Murdoch University, 2023). Try to operate a pulse-check system in these cases: check in with them to see how they are doing and encourage them to take a five-minute break if they indicate that they are becoming overwhelmed. Try to adopt a calm demeanour and embrace de-escalation tactics where possible:
>
> I would suggest things like simple de-escalation as well. When students get frustrated, when students get wound up, they're teenagers and they can be prone to dysregulation of their physical and emotional responses. It's about having that little bit of awareness and confidence to go 'right, we need to step it down' without this becoming a confrontation.
>
> Remember that it will often take time to build up strong support strategies that will work for your students. Take the time to get to know them and to learn about their specific triggers and patterns of behaviour. Be patient as you work with them and remember that 'they need time to trust you and time to kind of get in the zone'.

Remaining calm when responding to challenges of behaviour

For one of the LSAs I spoke to, remaining calm and not getting flustered was imperative when responding to cases of challenging student behaviour: 'The main thing is to keep calm and get them calm and (help them to) realise that they can trust you, and that no matter what happens, you are going to be the unshakable rock on which they can rely on'. Remaining calm in the face of challenging behaviour is particularly important in my own experience, as students can often mirror the behaviour that they witness from the adults around them, and it could cause them further stress and upset if they pick up on a sense of panic from their LSA.

> **Top tip:** Remember that it's okay to take a step back from a situation if a student's behaviour is becoming increasingly challenging or if you ever begin to feel personally unsafe: lean on a colleague or a manager to ensure that the student is safe, and take a step back to recalibrate if you feel overwhelmed. Responding to challenging behaviour can be immensely draining for educational support staff (Guikas & Morin, 2021), and it is important to recognise when you need to take a step back to protect your own wellbeing (see Chapter 2 for more tips on supporting your own wellbeing when working as an LSA).

It is similarly important to calmly set appropriate boundaries around acceptable behaviour. Use your own judgement to decide what you are not willing to accept, and be ready to calmly let a student know if they have crossed a line: 'If a student was rude to me or lied to me, I would act on that.' Be mindful too of what is a productive use of your time as an LSA. I have found that it's good to spend around 20 minutes helping a student to access their learning: check in with them to see how they are doing, and spend some time prompting, brainstorming and discussing key ideas and tasks. If after 20 minutes they are not engaging, then it's okay to take a short break to allow both you and them to recalibrate. Remember to make a log of the support you tried to give, so you have a clear record to refer back to, should you need to do so in the future.

Working with teachers to respond to challenges of behaviour: collaborative approaches and mutual support

A further element of LSA behavioural support stems from their work with teachers. LSAs can operate in a grey area when it comes to behavioural management responsibilities: many are keen to support their teaching colleagues in responding to challenging behaviour yet can be wary of adopting too much of a disciplinary role that could infringe on teacher authority in the classroom. Indeed, Clarke and Visser found that many TAs recognised their 'vital role in managing behaviour but [they also] noted the importance of "taking the lead from the teacher", being "low key" and supporting the teacher without "undermining them"' (Clarke & Visser, 2019, p.380). Other LSAs can also adopt more clear-cut boundaries when it comes to behavioural management: 'It's not the job of the LSA to tell a student off in a classroom for doing something that they shouldn't have done because that is the teacher's job.'

In light of the complexities of these working dynamics, a collaborative in-class approach between teachers and LSAs could be a good starting point when it comes to behavioural management. This is especially true given the stress that engaging with challenges of behaviour can cause for teachers. Repeatedly responding to disruption in class can be very draining, and it is vital that teachers have access to adequate training and in-class support in order to respond optimally.

I have found that teacher–LSA behavioural management strategies will often vary based on individual circumstances. The important thing is to communicate around these ahead of time, however, so they can be implemented seamlessly should the need arise during a lesson. For example, teachers and LSAs could devise a discreet system of behavioural management during lessons – a teacher may notice that a student is on the verge of becoming overwhelmed, for example, and could give an LSA a quick nod in order to indicate that they should support the student in accessing a rest break to help them calm down. This example of teacher–LSA collaboration would, in my view, be a good use of LSA time and teacher energy: the LSA could take the lead in managing the situation, minimising the risk of wider class disruption and enabling the teacher to keep their focus on the lesson.

My main advice for LSAs in this area would be to communicate with teachers in order to respond to the situations that are unfolding in front of you: check in with each other and share information where it is relevant. Establish yourself as a support for your teaching colleagues in class and let them know that you are on board to support them should they need some extra help. Don't hesitate to debrief with teachers after lessons, and to share your ideas about responding to challenges of pupil behaviour if you have any – the LSA has a unique vantage point in lessons and may be well placed to pick up on small details, such as discreet student phone use, that a teacher might miss. Share your ideas about managing situations, and work together to solve issues if they arise in class – more often than not, your teaching colleagues will be happy to have an extra form of support when it comes to behavioural management!

> Consider your work with teachers for a moment. Do you collaborate on issues of student behaviour in class? How might this collaborative aspect of your work be strengthened?

Navigating rejection as an LSA: respecting student preferences, taking a step back and exploring distanced and out-of-class support alternatives

A significant challenge of the LSA role can stem from student rejection, whereby students do not wish to work with an LSA in class and decline their support. It is first important to put this rejection in context and not take it personally. For many students, having an LSA with them in class marks a visible form of 'othering': it can be an indication to their peers that they require extra academic assistance, marking a form of significant social embarrassment for young people. Many LSAs reflected on their awareness of the social embarrassment that students may feel due to their presence in class: 'I think a lot of student rejection comes from their own personal feelings; they might think if someone's there with them [in class], they will stand out like a sore thumb.' For one LSA, it was particularly important to respect the views of young people regarding their preference for working with an LSA in class, as 'pushing in' and attending a class with a student who did not wish to work with them would be an unfair violation of their wishes: 'Sometimes they don't want to be the one with special needs or the one with an LSA, and if there's a student who really doesn't want you [with] them, I think you just have to respect that.'

Given the risk of social embarrassment and the need to respect student preferences, it is important for LSAs to be flexible when providing support to students who have declined their assistance in class. For one LSA, this meant actively **taking a step back** from their student and giving them as many opportunities as possible to work independently on chunks of their tasks:

> So I would always try not to be too closely attached. I would look in on them discreetly as often as possible, but not sitting with them and staring at everything they're doing. [I would] just check in every few

minutes and then, as long as we're getting on with the task, I'll be back in a few minutes. I'll come back and see how you're getting on. And [I would] just keep on checking in on them, but don't make it too heavy because some people would rather not have you too close to them for too much of a lesson. Try and move around, give them a break and keep on checking back– that's encouraging independence as well.

> **Top tip:** It's a good idea to provide clear scaffolded road maps to students who wish to work independently: this might mean ensuring a student has access to formula sheets or a checklist of steps to follow to help them to approach a task. You could also help a student to plan out their answers using a set teacher-approved format such as a Point, Evidence, Explain, Link to Question (PEEL) paragraph structure (University of Staffordshire, 2024), as shown in Figure 4.1.

In my experience of working with students who may be disinclined to accept LSA support, it can be useful to embed your support within a wider whole-class **floating** approach (see Chapter 5 for more details on the float method). Floating methods of in-class support are based on the idea that the LSA will 'float' across the class to support a range of students, as opposed to working solely with one pupil over the course of a lesson. Floating methods can be used optimally when they are directed by teachers, who give LSAs active direction about who to check in with for support. Often this method can work well for students who may feel embarrassed to work exclusively with an LSA in class, as floating creates the sense that the LSA is in the class to actively support all students – thus removing the focus from one individual. This was indeed true for one LSA, who noted:

> I float around and help other people as well, especially in subjects like Drama. In Drama, I was technically the LSA for one student, but he didn't want to stick out so I would help other kids sometimes as well if I got him started on something. Then I would just walk around the room and see [if other students] needed help, so then it wasn't clear that I was just there for one person. And I think that helped as well

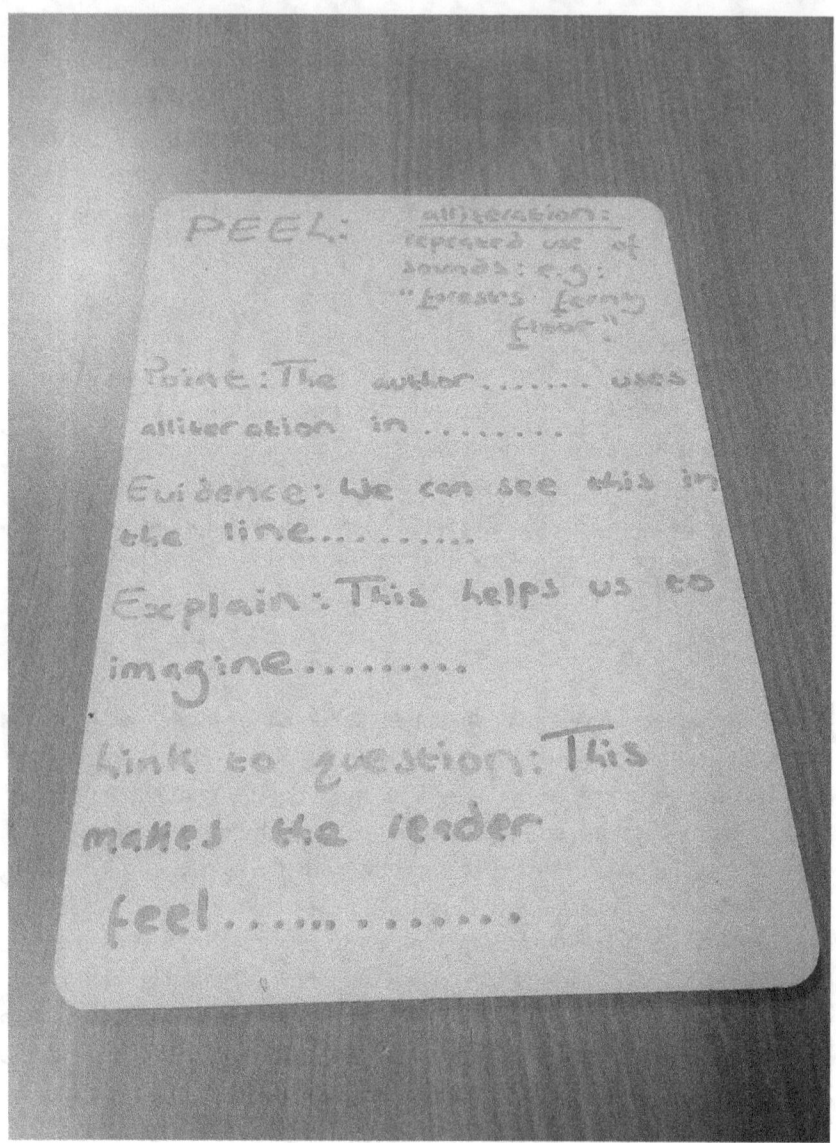

Figure 4.1 PEEL example

with communication with the teacher; she sort of introduced me in more of like a TA role than an LSA role, so she made it clear to the class that any of them could ask me questions, any of them could ask me for help. So that's always helpful if the teacher is guiding you through that class as well, then you know exactly what areas you can help with.

> **Top tip:** Liaise with teachers to ensure the float method is utilised optimally in class. There are numerous versions of implementing this method to support a mixed-ability class. One LSA noted that it may be useful for teachers to instruct LSAs to float in class to support higher-ability students in particular, to enable them to check in more actively with the students who may require extra help and guidance.

A further method of distanced LSA support that may be helpful to students who are hesitant to work with an LSA in class is **the check-in method** (see Chapter 5). This method has the advantage of enabling students to work independently to a large extent, whilst receiving structured support from LSAs. I have found it useful to layer the check-in method with online Teams support, frequently messaging students on Teams to see how they are progressing with their work so I can provide feedback and virtual support if they require assistance. For one LSA, such interactive technology was a useful means of supporting students academically without physically sitting in the classroom:

> I think one of the biggest benefits is the fact that you can interact from afar and you can give comments, you can encourage engagement in so many different ways and you can influence the work that comes out in the end.

Sometimes it may also work to reach an agreement with students whereby you do not sit next to them in class, but you provide note-taking support from the back of the room. This approach has the benefit of giving them their own **space** and soothing any concerns they have around social embarrassment, whilst also ensuring they are not left without support in class. Encourage them to take their own bullet-pointed notes during the lesson, and you can also provide them with a copy of more detailed notes after the class or via email.

There are multiple ways of addressing rejection as a LSA and it is vital to respect student preferences and to work with them to identify a type of support that they are comfortable receiving:

> I think there is also kind of a power in recognising the **autonomy** of the student and putting the power into their hands to have some level of influence in the kind of support that they feel is necessary or that they are happy receiving.

Remind students that future support will always be available, should they choose to access it: 'You can always just say no worries, but the door is always open if you do need help.'

It can often be good to present different options to students who are reluctant to engage with LSA support, and encourage them to reflect on the type of support that they would like to receive. Try to be flexible as an LSA here. It can be good to offer to trial different methods – such as weekly homework or coursework check-ins outside of class – so students have the opportunity to see what might work best in practice. Having a sense of choice is important for the self-efficacy of young people in education, and they are ultimately more likely to respond to some form of support if they feel that the LSA they are working with is a supportive and understanding person who is willing to respect their autonomy and preferences.

LSAs can thus respond to student rejection in numerous ways, including:

- Taking a step back/giving space
- In-class floating
- Distanced forms of LSA support
- The check-in method
- Respecting student preferences

> Consider the needs and preferences of your own students for a moment. Have they ever been unwilling to accept in-class support from an LSA? How might you work with them to identify alternative ways of supporting them that they might feel more comfortable with?

Supporting reluctant workers to engage: giving options, embracing student interests, building rapport and setting realistic expectations

Providing options and gentle encouragement: 'It's really giving the student the choice, especially at the post-16/17/18 level. They have to be treated more like adults who are capable of decision making'

LSAs, in addition to issues surrounding rejection, may commonly encounter challenges when it comes to student work reluctance. In these cases, it is often good to provide students with as many options as possible. Indeed, one former LSM noted:

> Probably the phrase I've said the most in learning support is something along the lines of 'it's not a great choice, but people like options'. It's basically this idea of saying, 'You can sit in the lesson or this teacher is going to give you a lunchtime detention and you're then going to have to start attending workshops, which are another lesson in your day that you're going to object to. It's not a great choice but which would you rather do?' So it's about that illusion of choice where they have a slightly objectionable option or a really objectionable option, and it's about asking well, which do you want? It's a really fantastic way of sometimes getting them to make a decision they might otherwise not make or avoid and cause themselves more problems.

Keep in mind that you sometimes will have to meet students halfway when you are working with them to navigate these issues: 'Right from the start, make it clear that it's not all or nothing.' Give students as many options and choices over the course of your work together and try to gently coax and persuade them when it comes to starting their work or attending their lessons to try to make things more manageable for them – in practice, this might mean suggesting something like trialling a lesson for 30 minutes and then going back out again for a short rest break.

It is thus useful to move away from ideas of an 'all or nothing' approach when supporting students to access their learning: try to diffuse pressurised situations by offering them flexible alternatives in a calm manner. For example, if a student is procrastinating or refusing to make a start with their work, you could suggest that they utilise a Pomodoro-style approach and attempt 15 minutes of a task, in recognition of the fact that 15 minutes' worth of effort is a useful starting point. Similarly, if a student is unwilling to attend their lesson, you can discuss different options and exit strategies with them. They could be given a rest break card for example, and reminded that they can take a five-minute break in an academic support department if they feel the need to over the course of a lesson. Gentle encouragement and support can also be offered in these situations – for example, by offering to walk a student to their lesson and checking in with them afterwards to see how it went.

> **Top tip:** Remember to provide support and reassurance to students if they are reluctant to attend a class: try to offer firm encouragement instead of reprimands, as this may cause further upset and stress for them.

Building rapport, enhancing the approachability factor and making learning as fun as possible

Other LSAs underscored the importance of creating **rapport** and a wider **approachability** factor when supporting students to engage with their work:

> It's about being approachable… when I start a [study] one-to-one session, I'll ask them how their week's been or if they did something over the weekend or something like that. It just eases them into it and you're not just throwing work straight away at them.

I have also found that it can be good to tailor your delivery of feedback, in the interests of strengthening your rapport with students. Some students may respond well to a more direct style of feedback, whilst others might prefer that you layer your feedback with positive reinforcement and questions ('That's a really interesting point. Have you considered the application of the feminist perspective in relation to this?'). Consider the preferences of your students here, and tailor your presentation of feedback accordingly.

Responding to challenging behaviour as an LSA

For two LSAs I spoke with, it was important to build **humour** and elements of **fun** into student work sessions, to create more enjoyable and engaging experiences for students who may initially be quite unwilling to get started with a piece of work:

> I think what works really well from my own experience is students will gravitate towards you more if you detail anecdotes that are humorous. I think a lot of it comes down to them possibly not knowing you. So it's the start of the year and they do not want to do any work at all and you're there with them. I feel like partially some of it is because you're sitting there and it makes them feel a little bit pressured to do something. I think it's about making sure that the student is comfortable with you, so you'll possibly [find out] what their special interests are – getting to know them properly is very important.

Often as you spend time with your students, you will develop a good understanding of their sense of humour:

> I think finding ways to relate work maybe to special interests and in terms of when they might just not want to work and have that motivation, if you find something that can motivate them and find ways to relate that back somehow, it does wonders. I had this one student who is very reluctant to do work sometimes. But just before this lesson, he was doing this funny accent activity with us. And this carried on sort of near the beginning of the class. I just said a question in one of the accents we were doing, and he found it hilarious. He was copying me, and he was working on an English task, so I said, why don't we read this passage in this accent and then see if you can find this thing in this accent? And he was doing so much work through that because he was having fun doing it.

Embracing student interests to support reluctant workers

For one LSA, weaving **student interests** into academic tasks was helpful in encouraging reluctant students to engage with their work. For this LSA, it was particularly important to take the time to appreciate what their students liked and were interested in, so their passions could be incorporated into academic tasks to pique student interests and to boost their attention:

> I think for me it's been a little bit kind of learn as you go, but it definitely is true that as you talk to a student and gradually understand more about them, it becomes easier to incorporate their interests or what they particularly gravitate towards just generally in the world into what it is that you might [be working on]. You might phrase particular questions if you're challenging them. I think particularly in the realm of English and creative writing, it can be a very powerful tool because there is that scope for the creativity of students to pick their own angles and very strongly incorporate what is personal to them. And I think that's a powerful thing because it becomes about them. And I think that if you can kind of build the world around them within the LSA sphere, I think that can be very powerful and very moving for a student.

The value of connecting with student interests was echoed by another LSA, who reflected that discussing student interests could sometimes be helpful to students who were struggling with issues such as school refusal or work avoidance. These discussions formed part of a wider supportive relationship within education, where they took time to **connect** with individual students:

> We have a lot of school refusers now, definitely more than we did pre-pandemic. And what we tend to do is just try and get them in the building and try and build up a relationship when they're in the building. Then you can slowly build up to going to a lesson or maybe sitting in the back [of the lesson] with them, and then slowly, they'll start to get into it. That's how I've always done it and I tend to be very good at having these [little] conversations that then link into what they're doing. So you have to get to know them, I think that's the most important thing.

For another LSA, wider discussions around **purpose** were helpful in encouraging students to engage with their studies:

> It's not always about the interest, it's about the need as well. So, for instance, [some] students may not understand the need to do a certain piece of work, because they [could struggle] to comprehend what the point of it is and therefore you hit a brick wall.

In these cases, wider discussions around the utility of the work itself can be fruitful, in helping the student to engage with wider questions of purpose. It may be good to focus on the specific skills that they could develop through engaging with the work here – for example, by encouraging them that they will develop literary and analytical skills by engaging with a piece of coursework. Be explicit about why the work is useful, and encourage your students to establish their own positionality in relation to a task.

> Consider the passions and interests of your own students here for a moment: what kind of things do they love to talk about? How could you draw on these passions to encourage them to engage with some academic tasks?

Nudging student behaviour and mirroring LSAs

Another LSA noted that it could be effective to gently nudge reluctant students towards their class or their studies, without explicitly telling them that they needed to go immediately. For them, it was particularly important to subtly and calmly **guide** students in the right direction:

> There are all sorts of things that I think people in education can do to steer people's behaviour benignly and it's as simple as just a comment such as 'Isn't it time you went to [class]' rather than 'You must [go]'. Because then you are phrasing it as a question and what you're not doing is becoming punitive about it and if [they] are really struggling, [you could say], 'OK, well, let's go together then.'

Indeed, another LSA noted that it was useful to work alongside their student whilst they were in a lesson, as the student had a habit of mirroring the LSA's behaviour when they saw them engaging with a piece of work:

> Often I find with some of my students who are quite reluctant, I'll just sit next to them and do some work and just be chatting to them and then I'll notice that they'll want to do some work too because I'm doing some work. It just sort of works.

> **Top tip:** It's important for LSAs to actively model pro-academic working habits in their working spaces that they share with students, as they are likely to pick up on and mirror the behaviours that they observe from the adults around them.

Effective study spaces and building routines

Effective study spaces mark an additional form of support for students who are struggling to engage with their work. We have a range of different academic support rooms in the department I work in, each of which is designed to support different ways of working – we have a quiet study room for silent working, as well as a collaborative working space that is supervised by LSAs for students who wish to discuss their work and engage in group study sessions. It's generally a good rule of thumb to ensure that study spaces are quiet and comfortable, and that distractions and socialising are kept to a minimum. It may also be a good idea to reach out to particular students who are struggling to engage with their work and to establish supervised study sessions with an LSA:

> In our department we have a study area and we invite [students] to come to study in our office study area so we can also monitor them or supervise them or encourage them to finish the homework or carry out the coursework or whatever it may be.

One LSA additionally noted that it was important to provide reluctant or struggling learners with set structures and routines when supporting them with their studies:

> They need their routine, so at the beginning we send them a weekly calendar, which helps them to organise themselves and improve their time management skills. I would [identify] free periods and I would tell them what they're going to do as catch-up homework. There was one student who is really reluctant to do homework at home and he's not

very productive when he's at home. Then we asked him, where do you feel most productive? He would go to a set place in college and he was able to crack on with his overdue homework and that was his way of learning.

> **Top tip:** See Figure 4.2 for a resource to help students at the secondary and sixth form level to organise their studies and set some weekly goals.

Time	Monday	Tuesday	Wednesday	Thursday	Friday
9:00 - 11:00	Maths		English	Maths	English
11:00 - 13:00		Music		Maths	
13:00 - 14:00			Film Studies		Art
14:00 - 15:00	Geography	French			
15:00 - 16:30				PE	Science

Weekly goals/revision priorities/targets

-
-
-
-
-
-

Figure 4.2 Weekly planning template

Setting realistic expectations

Finally, it is important for LSAs to set clear and realistic expectations around work for students. This could look like facilitating an open dialogue around the need for students to engage with their work, perhaps by making reference to the importance of personal commitment and a wider respect for student codes of conduct. It is important to be consistent with these expectations: it may be easy at times to 'give in' and allow students to disengage from their work, but this will not aid their prospects in the long term:

> They need to know that throughout life, they will have to do things that they don't always like or enjoy. It is just part of life. And we wouldn't be setting them up for life if we said, 'OK, you don't want to do that, let's not do it.' Life's not like that.

Top tip: It may be useful to trial student learner agreements here, perhaps ones that feature manageable study commitments for students to honour, such as 15 minutes of consistent work per day with an LSA in an academic support department. Work with your student to find a realistic commitment that will work for them and encourage them to engage with a voluntary student learner agreement to structure their work. I have also found it helpful on some occasions to encourage my students to take active ownership over their own learning. It may be good here to encourage them to reflect on their future ambitions: what would they like to achieve in the future and how might they use their current studies to bring these goals to fruition?

LSAs can thus draw on a range of strategies to support reluctant learners to engage, including:

- Providing options and gentle encouragement
- Encouraging routines and effective study spaces
- Embracing student interests
- Behavioural nudges
- Boosting the support and approachability factor
- Setting realistic expectations around work

Consider your own students for a moment. Have you ever encountered student work reluctance? How did you support your students to re-engage with their studies?

Mediative and restorative approaches to challenges of behaviour: bridging gaps of opinion as an LSA

For many LSAs, it can also be useful to adopt a mediative approach in order to bridge the gaps of opinion that can sometimes occur between students and their teachers. This, in many ways, reflects the liminal position of LSAs within education as they occupy a middle ground and sit somewhere in between students and teachers. For one former LSA I spoke to, their mediative role centred around considering student views and supporting them to feel heard in education:

> An LSA can act as a mediator by delving deeper into why a student doesn't want to do a particular piece of work, just to sort of understand where they're coming from. This can help you approach the task or maybe try and persuade the student to do the work. And I think this is a good way because it makes them feel like their opinions are valued, and again you can liaise with the teacher – speaking to both of them can definitely help come to a solution. I think what's important is that both parties, especially the student, feel like they're being heard. And I think building that rapport makes them more willing to try things that are out of their comfort zones.

> **Top tip:** Try to maintain a neutral standpoint when mediating differences of opinion as an LSA. Try to avoid the sense that you are 'taking a side' and maintain a solution-focused standpoint:
>
> Communication is very important in this job. If you can't convey why someone's opinion might differ to someone else's and explain why it might be conflicting to have certain opinions that conflict with another person, that will be very difficult. [You need to] be able to help a student or another staff member understand that having different opinions is alright. So, communication is key.

For one LSA, there was value to be found in adopting more of a restorative approach to their work with students. These approaches are orientated around rebuilding relationships when they have become strained:

> In educational and care settings, restorative approaches have been advocated by many as a means of bringing young people in conflict together, to undertake a deeper enquiry of the incident, including who has been affected and who is obliged to make amends, before agreeing their own long-term solution to the problem.
>
> (Sellman et al, 2014, p.1)

I have found over the course of my work that the LSA can at times play an effective role in helping students to repair their relationships with both teachers and peers, particularly if they have broken down due to instances of challenging behaviour. In these situations, it can be useful to meet with a student after a relationship has become strained: reflect on the situation calmly, as you re-examine it together. Try to encourage them to acknowledge their role in the situation and examine some restorative solutions such as an apology in the interests of moving on and future reconciliation.

Such a restorative approach was beneficial for one LSA I spoke to, who used their position as a student key worker to encourage their student to reflect on future solutions after a relationship had become strained:

> Particularly where you are a key worker as I was with that student, we had a meeting every couple of weeks. It helped to be able to go back to that student and say, 'Well, let's just rework that situation in a little meeting. Let's work to go back to that. What happened?' If that happens again, what are we going to do next? How are we going to do it differently? Having that sort of dialogue with them outside the classroom situation is really helpful.

I have found that an element of flexible and outside-the-box thinking can also be helpful in identifying solutions to resolve issues. Often it is good here to involve the student in decision-making processes as much as possible, to help them to feel a sense of active involvement and to avoid the impression that decisions regarding their academic work are being made by others. For example, if a student is reluctant to complete an in-class assignment, it may be fruitful to have a discussion with both the student and their teacher to suggest an alternative arrangement. Try to suggest some middle-ground solutions here, such as suggesting that the student complete the work at home or during a free period, emailing it to their teacher upon completion.

This is a small illustration of how LSAs can propose minor tweaks to a situation, to assist a student in achieving a key goal or outcome. Indeed, highlighting alternatives was an important aspect of mediation and student support for another LSA, who noted:

> [I would] say to the teacher, have you thought about this alternative? Rather than just going with the teacher's side and saying, 'Well, the student's in the wrong here', I would look at it a different way and suggest something like 'Can they work elsewhere? Can I work one to one with them, would that be better?' There are a number of spaces around our department that don't get used very often and I would say, 'Can we do a little bit of work in there, come back to you in about half an hour, see how we get on.' So I would try to come up with an alternative to that problem.

Finding solutions for primary school students: cool-down breaks, emotional regulation support and task chunking

There are additionally a number of support strategies that LSAs can utilise when managing pupil behaviour in primary schools. For one HLTA I spoke to, it was important to ensure that students were calm and happy in the classroom: 'If you're trying to work with that child, they also need to be in the right frame of mind to be able to access their learning.' It is important therefore to give students access to breaks from class if they need it, to ensure they can return at a later stage in an optimal frame of mind to continue with their work: 'I would give them brain breaks, to give that child time to regulate their emotions.'

For this participant, it was useful to incorporate calming activities such as breathing exercises into these student breaks, to support them in feeling calmer if they had experienced stress or unhappiness in class: 'Sometimes it's just stepping away from that classroom environment, just going to sit outside and thinking about practising some deep breathing or things like that.' They also noted that it could be particularly useful to merge task chunking with regular student breaks, to support students in engaging with structured and more manageable tasks:

'OK, this is what your teacher wants you to do' – maybe it's complete your math sheet. 'Let's chop up the worksheet into three sections, let's do this section first. Then we can go for a walk. After you've done that part, then we'll go back and do your second part.'

A calm and measured approach to managing student behaviour underpinned the practice of this HLTA, who noted:

Sometimes achieving that goal might just be done by taking a step at a time, by slowing it down a little bit and thinking about how the children need to feel like they've got someone on their side as well.

Concluding reflections

Managing challenging behaviour can be one of the hardest aspects of the LSA role: it is as draining for LSAs to respond to challenging behaviour as it is for teachers, with added complexity in view of the need for LSAs to have a strong working relationship with their students given the one-to-one working nature of the role. There are, however, numerous support strategies that LSAs can use to help students to manage their behaviour and emotions. Remember that you are not alone in managing behaviour: there are many people you can reach out to for support should you need it – teachers, line managers, SENCOs and other LSA colleagues. My time as an LSA has shown me that it's important to keep calm when dealing with challenging behaviour as there is a need to keep the relationship as humanised and as supportive as possible when students are presenting with challenging behaviour: listen to the student in question, find out why they are upset or stressed and use that information to support them in moving forward.

Try to move away from the idea of an 'all or nothing' approach to managing challenging behaviour, and keep in mind that it's okay for students to take a break and to return to their studies at a later point when they are in a better frame of mind to access their learning. It is similarly okay for you, as an LSA, to take a break from a challenging situation should you need to. Your wellbeing is also a priority, and it's important to recognise signs of overwhelm within yourself so you can take a step back from a challenging situation to recalibrate for five minutes if necessary (see Chapter 2 for more tips on supporting your wellbeing as an LSA). Ultimately, every student is different in how they will present with challenging behaviour, so it remains important to adopt a person-centred approach to behavioural management which addresses the specific needs and triggers of individual students.

> Consider your own students for a moment. What are some of their biggest behavioural challenges? What might an effective response look like in your view? Indeed, how might you best be supported as an LSA to meet the behavioural needs of your students?

References

Aas, H, K., Uthus, M., & Loire, A. (2023). Inclusive education for students with challenging behaviour: Development of teachers' beliefs and ideas for adaptations through Lesson Study. *European Journal of Special Needs Education 39*(1), 64–78. https://doi.org/10.1080/08856257.2023.2191107

Breyer, C., Lederer, J., & Gasteiger-Klicpera, B. (2021). Learning and support assistants in inclusive education: A transnational analysis of assistance services in Europe. *European Journal of Special Needs Education 36*(3), 344–357. https://doi.org/10.1080/08856257.2020.1754546

Clarke, E., & Visser, J. (2019). Teaching assistants managing behaviour – who knows how they do it? Agency is the answer. *Support for Learning 34*(4), 372–388. https://doi.org/10.1111/1467-9604.12273

Guikas, I., & Morin, D. (2021). Situation in special education: Interaction between teachers and children who have intellectual disability and who display challenging behaviours. *Canadian Journal of Education Revue Canadienne De l'éducation 44*(4), 1145–1175. https://doi.org/10.53967/cje-rce.v44i4.4937

Murdoch University. (2023, May 10). Warning signs your high school student is struggling. Murdoch University Blog: Raising Teenagers Series. www.murdoch.edu.au/news/series/series-articles/raising-teenagers/warning-signs-your-high-school-student-is-struggling

National Autistic Society. (2020, 14 August). Dealing with change - a guide for all audiences. The National Autistic Society. www.autism.org.uk/advice-and-guidance/topics/behaviour/dealing-with-change/all-audiences

Sellman, E., Cremin, H., & McCluskey, G. (2014). *Restorative approaches to conflict in schools: interdisciplinary perspectives on whole school approaches to managing relationships*. Routledge.

University of Staffordshire. (2024, November 29). PEEL Paragraphs: Academic Writing. Library and Learning Services. https://libguides.staffs.ac.uk/academic_writing/PEEL

5
Knowing when to take a step back: supporting student independence as an LSA

Chapter outline

Chapter 5 centres the importance of nurturing student independence as an LSA. I consider:

- The velcro LSA
- A holistic view of student independence
- The check-in method
- Dual-working approaches
- In-class note-taking strategies
- Float methods
- Seating arrangements, resource access and frequent check-ins
- Supporting students to get started
- One-to-one study independence
- Independence in primary working contexts
- A co-created approach to learning
- Embracing silences and knowing when to take a step back
- Honest learning conversations and the need to respect student preferences

The velcro LSA: 'It's all too easy to just slip into doing the work for them'

Velcro LSAs work too closely with their students (Skipp & Hopwood, 2019; Gerschel, 2005). Often they will sit continuously beside a student for the duration of a lesson, becoming overly involved with academic tasks (ETF, 2019). In practice, this could look like generating ideas or answering questions for a student, without their active engagement and the encouragement of independent thought. Velcro LSAs can inadvertently encourage pupil over-reliance, to the point where a student may expect an LSA to complete a task for them or disengage from a lesson because they know their LSA is taking notes for them. Indeed, one LSA noted:

> I don't like to be just sort of glued to one particular student, even if the only reason I'm in the classroom is because one child has the EHCP and so that's the justification for why it's on my timetable. But even in that situation, I don't want to just sit next to that person for the whole lesson. I want to be moving around and seeing what other people are doing and supporting a range of students. There is the danger that if the LSA is glued to the student with the EHCP, the teacher doesn't get to spend any time with that person and really the teacher should also be spending time with that person.

In light of these problematised aspects of the velcro LSA model, there is a need for LSAs to strike a delicate balance in ascertaining how and when to take a step back from a student they are supporting.

> Consider your own work as an LSA for a moment. Has a student ever become over-reliant over the course of your work together?

Adopting a holistic view of student independence: errands, travel training and the ladder effect

Pupil over-reliance can also percolate into the non-academic spheres of education when working as an LSA. Independence, for some students, may mean that they become accustomed to completing daily tasks, such as attending a meeting or getting a snack, without the prompting and guidance of LSAs. Independence for others may also crystallise around the social realm, as students pursue friendships and lean on LSAs less for their social connections within education. Student independence, whatever its form, marks an important form of progression for young people, and it's important that LSAs do not overstep the mark and inadvertently do too much for their students over the course of their work together. This was particularly important for one LSA I spoke with, who noted that LSAs may, at times, feel the need to justify their own existence and to work in an overly involved manner with students as a result:

> Do not overkill what you do in an attempt to justify your own existence. Standing back and letting a student struggle [a bit] is fine – as it is for a teacher. The art is to judge when intervention is necessary. This applies especially with older students.

Often when working as an LSA, I have found that it's been useful to ask myself: 'How might I reduce my input here, to maximise engagement and independent input from my student?' Make sure that you don't get drawn into completing small tasks for students who are capable: your job is to prepare them for the next step in their journey (be that secondary school, sixth form or university), and you therefore have a responsibility to support them to complete key tasks independently for themselves. For one LSA I spoke with, this clustered around encouraging a student to take ownership of their personal belongings:

> I had a student who would get upset in class and just run out, leave all his bags behind him and then he would say 'Can you go get my bags for me?' But from Year 10, I was like, no actually, I'm not going to go and carry your bags for you, we can walk there together and collect them. So then we also have talks about the fact that yes, you get upset, and yes, you need to leave, but then pick up your stuff and leave with it. Don't just leave it and then expect me to go back and pick it up for you.

Top tip: It's often good to work in incremental stages when supporting student independence. Don't withdraw your input and support abruptly as this may cause stress; instead, help your students to identify mini steps that will help them to reach their goal. Work with them to develop a plan of action, and gradually peel away your input as they progress. For one LSA, such an approach to supporting student independence was akin to a ladder effect, as they noted that:

Knowing when to take a step back: supporting student independence

> I think small steps would be good and to have almost like a ladder effect: you start at the bottom and work your way up with the independence, setting certain goals for students to achieve, put a timeline to them. To start off with, you can support the student doing something for the first few times so they can get used to what they need to do and so they can feel comfortable with where they need to go and how they need to go about this.

LSAs can also support student independence when it comes to wider life skills such as journey planning and travel logistics.

> **Top tip:** It may also be fruitful to weave training opportunities into student events and activities. If you are accompanying a student on a school trip, for example, that may be a good opportunity to build in a form of travel training to boost their skills and independence when it comes to navigating public spaces and modes of public transport.

The check-in method

The check-in method can work well for LSAs in sixth form college contexts, particularly for creative subjects that have practical and self-directed components such as Media and Art. This method consists of a number of steps:

- First, accompany your student to their class to ensure they arrive on time.
- Stay in the class for the first 10–15 minutes, and ensure the student clearly understands the task at hand. You can check their understanding by asking them to articulate what they plan to do over the course of the lesson. Bear in mind that some students may say that they are fine during the lesson, but it's important to hear an outline of their work plan before leaving the check-in session. You can always help them to craft a checklist of steps to follow if they seem unsure (see Figure 5.1 for more details), and you can always liaise with teachers to produce a clear written 'lesson goal' to ensure students remain on track with their work.

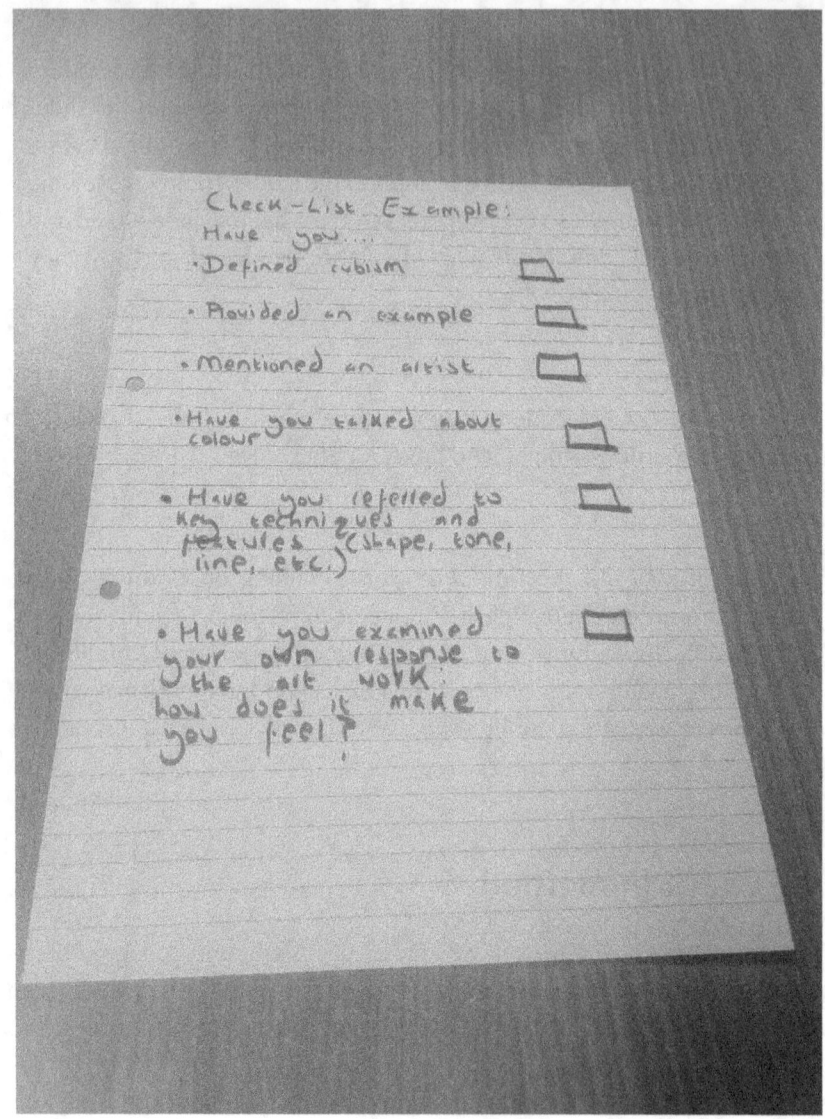

Figure 5.1 Checklist example

- Once you are happy that the student is confident with their process and their next steps, leave the class, checking back in frequently for updates on their progress.

> **Top tip:** Layer this method with virtual check-in support via Microsoft Teams. This can be easily implemented as you are leaving the class, by telling the student to message you on Teams if they need any help. It's also important to let your teaching colleagues know that you are trialling this method, so they are kept in the loop as to why you are entering and exiting the classroom at regular intervals.

The check-in method has numerous advantages when it comes to supporting student independence. It gives them physical space away from their LSA, presenting them with opportunities to work in a manner that is largely self-directed. Having this physical space away from LSAs is especially important given factors such as social embarrassment. Certain students who are entitled to LSA support may be concerned that it makes them stand out from their peers: 'This is their teenage life. They don't want a middle-aged woman sitting next to them. They don't want that at all.' Indeed, some students can understandably feel uncomfortable if an LSA continuously sits next to them in class; the check-in/online Teams support method can work well for students who may be on the brink of LSA refusal due to fears of peer judgement and social embarrassment.

This method also has particular benefits when it comes to supporting students in their creative flow:

> For creative subjects such as Media or Art or Drama or Music, there will be times where you will be in that lesson and they will be doing their own thing, such as acting or filming or art. And while you are assigned to that student, I feel that whenever they do a subject that allows them to [cultivate] a creative mindset, in order for them to really feel that independence and to have that full creativity, it would be better if you told them: if you need me, just message me on Teams or email me and I will come back. I will let you do your own thing. And hopefully when I come back to check on you, you can report back to

me on how it's going. And then if everything's alright, you can leave them again. And you can come back at the end of the lesson just to say how did it go, do you want to show me anything? And most of the time, they will have stuff to show you.

I have found that it is sometimes very important to take a step back when supporting students, and to gauge when is appropriate to pitch your ideas and input. Students will, under certain circumstances, need time to experiment with their peers as they trial different methods and creative strategies. This can be particularly true in areas such as the dramatic arts. One LSA I spoke with reflected:

> You really find independence and social skills, especially in Drama. It's not great to have someone that's watching what you're doing because that's your time to have free rein, so to speak, to speak with people and really build that independence up for yourself.

One LSA I spoke with felt that the check-in method had specific benefits in sixth form working contexts, as it can help to prepare students for future university studies by exposing them to pockets of independent work in a structured and supportive manner:

> I think it's also really important especially in a sixth form setting, since this is the stepping stone to university, you won't have as much help there, per se. So giving them the chance to work on their own for a bit and seeing how they handle it [is useful]. And if they do want to go to university, it's a really good way of them getting used to us not being there.

This method additionally has benefits when it comes to LSA working time, as the gaps between check-ins can enable LSAs to catch up on admin tasks and emails over the course of the day:

> We can then plan one-to-one support sessions with other students or if there are students that have a free and are doing coursework, you can watch over them at the same time as going to check in on the others.

Finally, it is important to put this method of independent learning support in context. It can work with subjects that have a self-directed, creative, often practical component. It could be used optimally in an art or a graphics class, for example, where a student can work independently in a creative flow on a project that involves something like ink drawing or painting. This method also depends on the needs of individual students, as some students may have certain needs that require more consistent levels of LSA support in class. It can work well under the right circumstances, however (e.g. you support consistently for theory-based lessons and check in for practicals), and herein lies the importance of individual judgement.

The check-in method thus has numerous advantages, including:

- Giving students space to pursue independent work
- Supporting creative flow and student experimentation
- Future university preparedness

> Consider your own work as an LSA for a moment. Might the check-in method work for any of the students you work with?

Dual-working approaches

Dual approaches to LSA–student working can also work well at secondary and sixth form level. These approaches are structured as follows:

- Sit with your student and identify a set task to work on (e.g. a Maths or an essay question).
- Work with them to structure a response to the question (i.e. discuss a mathematical formula or draft an essay plan).
- Complete your own answer to the question, whilst your student completes theirs.
- Compare both answers at the end of the session, discussing each approach and providing reciprocal feedback.

This method can benefit students as it encourages them to independently apply their subject knowledge to practice questions, in a manner that is constructive and supported. Students can also feel quite motivated to work on a question alongside an LSA, and adopting such a dual method of working can create a sense of camaraderie for students who may struggle to practise exam questions on their own. This method works especially well if an LSA has a particular subject specialism (I have been able to use my knowledge of sociology, for example, to answer past paper essay questions alongside students). This method can work for a range of subjects, as one TSA used this method for Maths revision with their student, noting:

> I have a student and I let him work independently. [We kind of work alongside each other], he does maths and I do maths and then we can compare notes after each page to see who's got the right answer. And it's not always me, I don't mind making mistakes. That makes you more realistic because I don't know 100% of everything in maths. I absolutely don't. I do make mistakes and so we compare notes. That allows them to work independently to an extent.

In-class note-taking strategies

A further component of student independence stems from LSA approaches to in-class note-taking. There is a risk that a small number of students may over-rely on an LSA to take notes in class, whilst others may disengage from their studies when their LSA is beside them taking notes:

> Some students really, really want you to just write everything for them and ultimately that won't help because even if you get the notes in their book, those students are probably not going to actually do anything with those when they get home or find them useful when they come to revise for an exam or anything like that.

A good strategy to combat these risks can be to encourage your students to jot down some key bullet points in class, whilst you focus on the more detailed subject notes – let them know that you will cover the granular detail, but encourage them to take a few notes over the course of the lesson as well. It can be useful to prompt students when note-taking as an LSA, encouraging them to jot down some key ideas where possible: 'I'll sit and prompt kids "you should be making notes here".'

Knowing when to take a step back: supporting student independence

Try to give your students guidance on how to organise their own notes in class: 'I'll give them a little bit of guidance on how to structure their notes – so here's some headings or we could lay it out like this etc.' You may wish to try a Cornell style of note-taking (Pauk & Owens, 2010), leaving a summary box at the end of the page for them to fill with their own thoughts and ideas (see Figure 5.2 for more details).

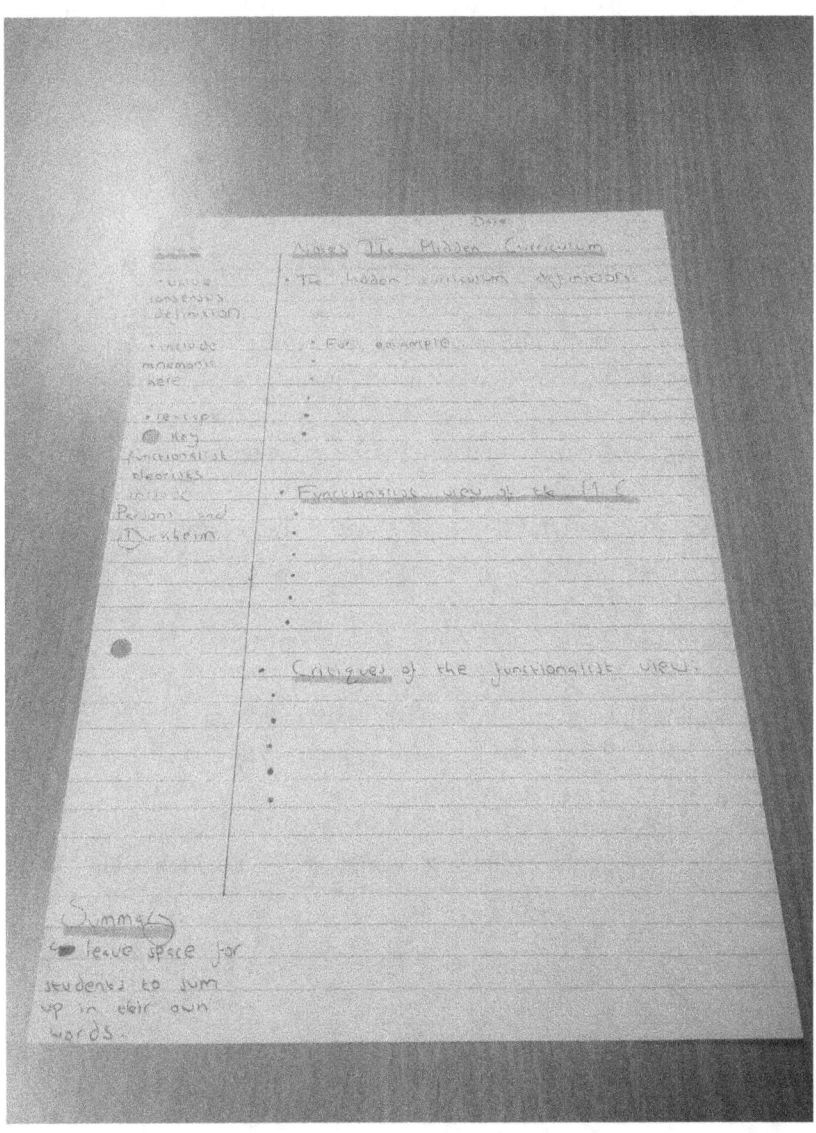

Figure 5.2 Cornell notes (Pauk & Owens, 2010) example

Another former LSM also mentioned the importance of active student direction and engagement when it comes to in-class note-taking:

> When I was regularly supporting in lessons, there was kind of a very clear dialogue between me and the students [around note-taking]. It would be things like if it is an objective fact, if the teacher is saying this is the case, I will get that down in your notes. That is going to be there. But if you are watching a video and the teacher says to make notes or if it's English and we are reading a script and annotating it. You need to tell me, 'Can you make a note of that?' [You have to put] as much of that onus on them to be like 'This is something I want in my notes and this is something I don't'.

Finally, it is important for students to review their notes at regular intervals:

> I've also made reams and reams and reams of electronic notes, and they've never checked them once, and that starts to question what's the validity of my notes, of that support because if they're going to make notes and not refer to it, am I wasting my time?

Try to schedule regular check-ins with them to discuss and review notes, to ensure they are getting the most value out of the LSA support that is available for them.

LSAs can thus support note-taking independence by:

- Encouraging students to jot down key bullet points
- Prompting students to note-take where appropriate
- Giving clear note-taking guidance
- Encouraging students to direct LSA note-taking in class
- Regularly viewing notes to ensure engagement and added value

> Consider your own in-class note-taking approaches for a moment. How might you refine them, to foster more active input from your students?

Float methods

In-class floating, where LSAs assist numerous students in a class, can also help to support pockets of in-class independence for students:

> We have that one [EHCP] student that we're there for but then there's a handful of other students in that class that also have been highlighted as needing support. And so we really sort of chop and change between who we go to and who we support.

One participant noted that this approach was suitable for one of their students in particular:

> [She's] quite independent. I sit away from her, I let her go with the task. If she needs me, she knows I'm there but she doesn't need me next to her. Now I can help some of the children keep on [task]. I always say to the teacher, 'I'm here for this child, but I'm going to float around the whole class.'

For one TSA, a float method of support worked well when they identified another student in the class who needed extra support:

> I will work around the room at the start of term and I'll find a student that's weaker than the other students and then I'll bounce off that student to my student. So that gives my student [with the EHCP] a break and then [the other student] actually gets a bit of support. That's how I've always done things because then the student I'm with doesn't feel like I'm on them all the time and [they] also get to work independently and they get to be teenagers.

Floating in class as an LSA has the advantage of enabling LSAs to provide support to a broader range of students (many of whom may not have an EHCP). It can be useful to liaise with teachers to check their SEND register here, so you can target your floating in class. I have also found that it can work to pose questions to different groups of students when floating in class: try to encourage group discussion where possible, to avoid the focus being placed too heavily on a single individual.

> **Top tip:** Pair in-class floating approaches with clear teacher-approved task direction. Ensure the student has clear task understanding and provide a road map to approach the work if needed. For example, if you are supporting a GCSE English student, work together to plan out a Point, Evidence, Explain, Link to Question (University of Staffordshire, 2024) paragraph structure (see Figure 4.1), highlighting the evidence that could be used in the text to support their key point. Once the student is set to begin their task, you can then tell them that you are going to float around the class to see how other people are getting on with their work, and that you will be back afterwards to see how they have got on.

Floating as an LSA often works well in lessons when there is direction from teachers, as they will often have a good understanding of where the class is at and where there may be particular gaps in people's knowledge. (See Chapter 3 for further reflections on how LSAs can work well with teachers for the benefit of all students in class.)

A further advantage of floating in lessons was also summed up by one LSA I spoke with, who reflected:

> Normally, what I start off by doing is helping other people in the class so that I don't look like I'm just there for [one particular student]. Because I think sometimes they get really nervous that they're going to be obvious as 'the EHCP' in the room. Whereas if you're just helping the other kids and then you slowly sort of circle back to them, they can start to think, 'Oh, okay, she's just helping everyone.'

It was also noted that in-class floating methods can gradually be extended over time to boost student independence:

> I'll say to them just have a go at it, do one or two questions, I'll come back and then we'll do it again. We'll keep doing it. And then gradually the length of time gets longer and longer and longer and hopefully that eventually leads to them being able to just pop their hand up when they need help.

One TSA I spoke with also found it useful to provide as little input as possible when initially working with a student in class, checking in with them regularly and providing further support as and when was needed: 'Try and do as little as possible [in the beginning]. Leave them to it and float around and just be available to them if they do need you again. But try and get them to be more independent.'

Some key elements of effective floating can thus include:

- Identifying a student who needs extra help and floating between them and your assigned student
- Working with teachers to ensure effective floating
- Providing students with clear, teacher-approved task direction as you float to support their peers
- Checking a class SEND register to target LSA floating support

> Consider your own LSA working context for a moment. How might you utilise, or refine, a floating method to support the needs of your students?

Supporting in-class independence: seating arrangements, giving space, frequent check-ins and resource access

Certain in-class factors can also contribute to greater levels of student independence. It's really important to give students **space** as and when they need it, as some may feel uncomfortable and overly observed by the continuous input of an LSA in class. **Seating** was highlighted by one LSA as a key factor here, as having physical distance away from their student was helpful in cultivating a greater sense of independence: 'I sit away from her, I let her go with the task. [If] she needs me, I'll be there.' Sitting apart from a student can thus be helpful in subverting velcro LSA models where an LSA is glued to a single student for an extended period of time in class. When sitting away from students, it is important to ensure they are equipped with clear direction and adequate in-class resources to work independently for chunks of time away from an LSA. Indeed, one HLTA noted:

[I make] lots of **word banks** for the children that they can look back on. I know with a phonics group that I was working with last year, they all ended up having phonics dictionaries, so together we made little phonics dictionaries and things like that. So then when they went back to class, they still had that resource that they could then use to help them with their literacy when they were in class. So all those kind of things, **help sheets and prompts** that children can use independently once they've been taught how to use them, they promote that independence and then it just makes them feel better, I think because then they feel like they're like everyone else. They don't need somebody to be sat with them. They just need to be shown how to use those things so that they can then implement it into their work.

In-class resources are thus important components of student independence. Such resources can additionally include help sheets, definition cards or formula sheets, and it can often be a good approach to work alongside a student to identify what works best in support of their independent learning (e.g. some students may work well in class when provided with a clear checklist that breaks tasks down into individual steps).

Finally, it is important to use your judgement when structuring blocks of independent working time for students in class, as there may be some cases – for example, if a student has certain scribing requirements – where more consistent levels of LSA support are required. **Pulse-check** what you feel your students need, and structure your in-class support accordingly. Try also to encourage your students to take ownership of their learning and to reach out for help as and when they need it in class – encourage them to vocalise what they need during class, by requesting resources or seeking further explanation from their teacher if there is something they are unsure about.

LSAs can thus trial the following approaches to boost student independence in class:

- Sitting away from students
- Providing them with resources such as word banks, help sheets and formula sheets
- Encouraging students to take ownership over their learning and to vocalise when they require extra help from teachers

> Consider your own students and their needs for a moment. What methods might work best to support their in-class independence?

Supporting students to get started: exemplar answers, filling in the blanks, give it a go and positive reinforcement

Getting started with a piece of work can be challenging for many students, especially at sixth form level when they are faced with the ongoing demands of A Level and BTEC qualifications. If a student is struggling to begin an essay or a particular set of questions, encourage them to initially write down everything they know about the topic – assist them with this **brainstorm**, as jotting down some initial ideas might help them to get into the flow of writing. You can also work with them in a one-to-one study session to review their notes and to recap key concepts using their textbook: help them to identify any key gaps in their knowledge, and signpost them to their teachers for further support (there is no expectation that an LSA will be able to fill subject-specific knowledge gaps during one-to-one study support sessions). It is finally useful for LSAs to help students to make **plans** to tackle key essays if they are struggling to make a start with their work: engage in a dialogue with them to hear their initial ideas and reach out to subject teachers to request essay planning frames that you can use to help them with their initial plans.

One TSA found that it was especially useful to provide students with **exemplar answers** and clear outlines of key tasks in order to aid students with task initiation:

> What helps a lot with students is that I give them a skeleton outline of what's required. So many of them don't understand the task itself, so they don't see what the end result is. There are very few tutors that say, for instance, I want you to design a poster but they won't have 2/3/4 examples of what they're looking for. So the general class will kind of fumble their way in the dark and find something. But for your supported student, they don't know where to start or what the end result is going to be. So often giving them a skeleton outline of where they're going and what they should be doing [is helpful]; And then you can

gradually say, okay, so find a piece of A4 paper, tick. You've done that all right. Let's go on to the next step. And so making things a little more structured but not giving them the answers has often worked for me.

> **Top tip:** Always reach out to teachers if you need materials such as this, as they will often have a plethora of helpful resources that you can draw on to help students with their work.

One LSA I spoke with also reflected on the value of using a mini whiteboard in class: 'My most useful piece of equipment that I always use is a tiny little whiteboard. I find it's especially helpful in Maths.'

> **Top tip:** Bring a mini whiteboard to class and write out some core elements of a written task – such as a Point, Evidence, Explain, Link to Question paragraph structure (University of Staffordshire, 2024) – and leave blanks for a student to fill in and consider. This technique can be especially helpful for students who struggle to begin with their work. I have also found it useful to provide students with sentence starters if they are struggling to start a piece of written work. These sentence starters are subject specific but an example could include something like: 'The writer effectively utilises alliteration over the course of the text, as is reflected in the following sentence...' Encourage your student to fill in the blanks using their own words, and provide them with a written definition of the word 'alliteration', so they can refer back to it should they need a key terminology recap.

Another participant found that a **'give it a go'** technique was useful in prompting students to take a stab at independent work, as they would encourage their students to 'try these two questions on your own, then I'll come back to you and we'll check and see how they're doing'.

> **Top tip:** Give verbal support and encouragement to students to support their efforts at independent work and task management – this can even include praising seemingly small steps, such as a solo trip that they make to a canteen or classroom. Indeed, the importance of positive reinforcement for student efforts was summed up by an LSA as they reflected that:
>
> There's motivation, encouragement, praise for small things that they manage to do independently, so that gets reinforced when they've done a small piece of work by themselves and I praise them for it, they're pleased with themselves and want to do it again a little bit more next time.
>
> Remember that certain students may also experience praise as a stressful demand, so temper this approach in light of your knowledge of the students you work with.

LSAs can thus utilise a range of strategies to help students make a start with their work, including:

- Initial brainstorms
- Essay planning support
- Exemplar answers and skeleton outlines of tasks
- Filling in the blanks
- The 'give it a go' technique
- Verbal encouragement and support

Promoting independence during one-to-one study sessions: timers and student revision resources

There are additionally a number of strategies that LSAs can utilise to support student independence within one-to-one study sessions. A good starting point here concerns the use of **timers**. One HLTA noted that they would sometimes use timers to encourage their students to engage with a structured segment of their work: 'Timers [can be useful] by saying "See how many sentences you can get done by the time I get back. I'll come and check on you after your three-minute timer has gone off.'" Timers are useful in adding structure to segments of independent work, and it's useful to bear in mind that even 15 minutes of work from a student is worth acknowledging and reinforcing positively. One-to-one sessions can also be useful spaces for LSAs to dedicate specific blocks of time to individual student revision needs, and I have found it useful to focus on practice questions and exam past papers as often as possible to help familiarise students with their formal assessments.

Try also to empower your students to find the study methods that work for them – be that through speech-to-text software or through the creation of visually pleasing mind maps or colour-coded notes. Let them know that a traditional reading and writing approach to learning (Fleming, 1995) is not the only way to structure their studies, and encourage them to reflect on the methods that may be optimal for them. Often it can be good to provide **options** and examples here, perhaps by drawing on VARK (Visual, Auditory, Reading and Writing and Kinaesthetic) learning theory to aid them with this exploration – be sure to use the phrase 'learning preferences' when engaging in this exploration, and to let them know that their learning 'style' is by no means set in stone. There have been numerous critiques of VARK learning theory (Husmann & O'Loughlin, 2019), and it is therefore best used as a tool to promote reflection around what might work, as opposed to guiding students towards a set 'learning style'.

> **Top tip:** It's a good idea to incorporate student exam access arrangements into one-to-one sessions as much as possible, as this will help students to refine exam techniques and make optimal use of readers, scribes and prompters. It is finally important that learning within one-to-one sessions is largely directed by students, and that they actively participate in the creation of their own revision materials. Providing templates, such as bullet-pointed revision note cards and mind maps, can be a good place to start in helping students to create resources that will work for them.

It can also often be good to help students to break down key tasks into manageable chunks over the course of your one-to-one sessions together – see task breakdown sheet (Figure 5.3) for more details.

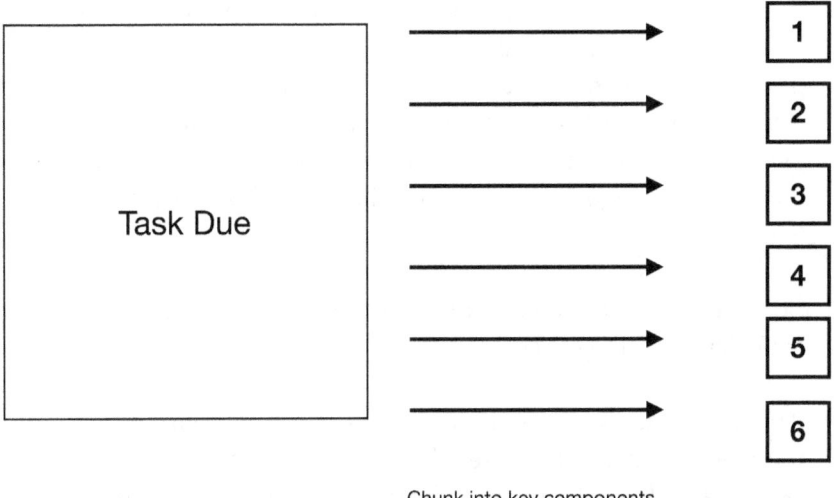

Figure 5.3 Task breakdown sheet

For example: an essay could be due, and you could break it down into the following key components:

- Introduction
- Paragraphs 1–4
- Conclusion

Remember to make sure that the student has a clear sense of what will be explored in each component of the task – for example, paragraph 1 will examine the economic factors that contributed to a key historical event. Work with the student using a calendar or their timetable to plan when they will work on each task component over the course of the upcoming week.

Supporting independence in primary school contexts: task boards and turn-taking

Although levels of student independence vary significantly across primary, secondary and sixth form contexts, there are a range of strategies that LSAs can use to boost pupil engagement in primary schools:

> In reception, it's about helping them to be much more independent in their actual life skills. How they're looking after themselves, how they're **making friends**, how they're **sharing**, how they're **taking turns**. It's about helping them so that as they are going into Year 1, they are much more prepared to sit down and do some work by themselves or work on a project just with other children without having an adult with them.

For one HLTA I spoke with, task boards were useful in supporting student independence at primary level:

> I use lots of **task boards** with the children that I work with. So, one that I use at the minute, it's broken down into five parts. If it's Maths, for example, first, you lay out your question and you kind of break down [each] step for them so the children don't actually need me, they can follow their task board, but they just need somebody to be there to write out the steps for them so that then they can make that accessible. Then that way I can go and support other children, as well as still keep an eye on that child and then I can check in on them later and address any miscommunications or bits that they've got the wrong end of the stick with.

A co-created approach to learning: student–LSA collaboration and paired student learning

A useful frame for fostering student independence stems from a conceptualisation of learning as a co-creation. Co-created learning is equitable and democratic in nature: learning is not a process that is 'done to students'; it is instead one that they actively participate in and have the ability to influence (Bovill, 2020; Shor, 1992). When learning is repositioned as a co-created practice in education, it becomes one that the LSA and the student can actively engage in together as they **work collectively** to reach higher planes of understanding. A reconsideration of hierarchical LSA–student frames, whereby an LSA fully directs student learning experiences, can thus be a useful exercise in empowering students to actively influence pockets of their own learning. Often this can occur in practice by encouraging students to explain concepts and ideas to their LSAs, in support of their academic and communication skills.

One LSA touched upon this frame of learning as a co-creative practice when they reflected on an instance when their student showed them how to use a website during a class: 'It's equal parts them learning about how to use the website and equal parts me learning how to use the website.' This is an interesting view of student learning within a co-creative frame as it was a collaborative process whereby the student and the LSA worked together as a team to complete a task. It is fundamentally a good approach to be open to learning from your students, as empowering them to explain concepts and ideas for themselves fosters both co-creative learning approaches and skills of articulation and oratory.

Co-creative learning approaches can also flourish through student **paired learning** and inter-student teaching strategies, which foster a more equal playing field between students. Often LSAs can act as facilitators within these approaches by encouraging students to work together. For one HLTA, pairing students up to work on a task together was a good way to prompt them to make a start on their work: 'I [use] partners as well: so-and-so is going to write this part. OK, now you can have a go at this bit.'

> **Top tip:** It is good practice to clearly structure student group work activities, ensuring that all students are aware of a clear group work goal and that they each have strongly defined roles and activities to work on within the group project. Keep tabs on the group as they work together, ensuring that they stay on task and do not veer too far off-topic.

These paired learning strategies have additional benefits when it comes to fostering an independent approach to student work, as they can reduce over-reliance on an LSA by ensuring that students work **collaboratively** together to complete a set task without the need for consistent LSA input. This approach was valuable for one LSA I spoke with, who noted: 'I asked this particular student who luckily sat next to us and she was very helpful and she was willing to work in a pair with my student and he worked very well with that experience together.' Often it can be good to use your own knowledge of a class to select a supportive peer for your student to pair up with – be attuned to who might work well with them, and slowly peel back your support once they have got the ball rolling with their work.

Knowing when to take a step back: embracing silences, leaving space for mistakes and resisting the urge to over-correct

For one TSA, embracing silence was an integral element of supporting their students in engaging with their work independently:

> It's really, really hard to step back, it's hard to stand there doing nothing and it's hard to stand there not saying anything. It really takes practice and experience to know when to [keep quiet] to be honest and sometimes you can over-talk. So it is like a dance, it's like you have to dance between being there and being supportive and not helping and saying 'You can do it'.

This idea of **dancing with silence** resonates strongly for me throughout my own practice as an LSA. There have been many instances where I have worked with a student in class and significant silences have emerged when I have asked them questions to prompt their thinking on a particular topic. My instinct has been to fill these gaps, often with more questions, which can, in turn, create confusion for students.

It is important to remember that many students with SEND requirements may have varying **processing speeds**, meaning they may require longer periods of time to consider a question. It is thus good practice to embrace student silence when supporting students as an LSA, and to resist filling gaps of silence when they emerge with ideas and further questions. It can be beneficial, instead, to lean into these silences: let students be silent and consider a question for up to a full minute, after which time you can check in with them to gauge their understanding. Once a student has been given adequate time to consider the question for themselves, LSAs can then offer some assistance by asking a question such as 'Would you like me to suggest a sentence starter?' or 'Would you like me to rephrase the question?'

This TSA also highlighted the importance of allowing students to make mistakes, and of resisting the urge to **over-correct** a student who was on the wrong track when answering a question: 'Another thing that's very important is to let students make mistakes. It's probably not a very popular thing to say but it's 100% OK to watch them make mistakes.' For this LSA, student mistakes were integral to the process of learning, as it was through examining where – and why – a student went wrong that they could eventually reach a higher plane of understanding: 'OK, why did you do that? What did you think when you did that? OK, let's look at [this]; you've got the right process and method, but still the numbers are wrong.' Student mistakes can thus mark a valuable part of the learning process, as it is through considering student errors that LSAs can facilitate deeper conversations to examine where exactly a student has gone wrong.

It's worth bearing in mind that sometimes **less can be more** as an LSA:

> My general assumption is that I won't intervene unless I'm needed. There are people who will jump in much quicker and start organising everything for the student. Sit, watch and wait and see how a student is doing, do not jump in and start doing it for them.

Let your students know that you will always be there to help, but be sure to give them time to process, think and reflect for themselves. Be careful not to over-question them over the course of your work together, as it's important that they develop an independent approach to their work:

> I think you've got to be willing to walk away from them for a bit. I think if you sit there and go 'What's your next sentence going to be?' then they're going to get so reliant. We definitely had some students that got too reliant on us in Year 7.

Remember also to avoid things such as reading over their shoulder when they are producing work, as this could make them feel distracted and overly observed in class.

The worst thing you can do as an LSA is to push and prompt a student when they are not in an optimal headspace to engage with their learning – pushing too hard risks straining the working relationship that you have: give space, take a step back, give the student a break and let them know you will be there if they feel more ready to engage with their work. It is finally important to encourage a sense of **ownership** when it comes to student learning: engaging with their learning is ultimately their responsibility – especially at sixth form level – and it's important to bear this in mind over the course of your work together as an LSA:

> If we picture that student as a motor car, we're not there as the driver: we're the navigator, so we can point them in the right direction and then we can support with what to do, where to go, how to do it? But ultimately, it's got to come from the student. Slowly, we can work with those students and from the outset start to get on to the level to gradually motivate them, and if it's still not working, then it's not working and I think too many of us take it personally. If a student doesn't want to work, it's not our fault. The minute they do want to work, we're behind them 100%, but ultimately, it's up to them.

LSAs can take a range of approaches in support of student independence, including:

- Embracing silences
- Reducing the urge to over-correct student errors
- Saving interventions for when they are needed
- Giving students space and not over-prompting them, or reading over their shoulders during class

Respecting student autonomy: making space for student choices and facilitating honest learning conversations

It is useful to bear in mind that each of these methods, from dual-working approaches to student check-ins, will be suitable for students on the basis of their individual learning requirements and abilities. A good rule of thumb when developing your working practice is thus to check in regularly with students, to ascertain what their needs and **preferences** are. For one LSA working at sixth form level, this meant meeting with their student to discuss support strategies and potential points of improvement:

> Every year when we get our timetable and our new students, the first thing I do is I say, 'Right, you're now in the post-16 environment. Tell

me how you want to be supported.' So I actually put the ownership back on to them because all their life in primary school, in secondary school, they've been told how the support was going to be and 'It's going to be like this, this is how we're doing it. You don't have a say in it.' So I actually put the ownership on to them and I ask them, 'How do you want to be supported?' So I'll just say, you can think about it and then we'll work it out between you and me, how we're going to do it. But ultimately you have to do the work. So it's about having that conversation about how they want to be supported and reminding them as well they are here to do the work.

Young people are ultimately very good judges of the support that works best for them, and it is important that their autonomy and preferences are respected through **learning conversations** that seek to ascertain their views on what will work well for them when it comes to their in-class support:

I think there is kind of a power in recognising the autonomy of the student and putting the power into their hands to have some level of influence in the kind of support that they feel is necessary or that they are happy receiving. I've received some feedback in the past about myself about potentially being too overbearing towards particular students.

> **Top tip:** Layer open-ended check-in questions like 'What support might work best for you?' with specific examples, as certain students may not be sure of the options that are available to them in terms of their in-class support. You could layer these questions with specific examples – 'Would you like me to check in for X subject, or would you prefer for me to adopt more of an in-class float approach?' These conversations may also be a good way to discuss trialling different methods of support, so students will be able to gain a clearer sense of what may work well for them in practice. It's also a good idea to check in with your students around their EHCP outcomes. It's really important that they know what these outcomes are, and that you welcome open dialogue around how you will work together in support of their outcomes.

> Consider your own students for a moment. What methods might work best for them in terms of in-class support, and how might you approach these learning conversations to ensure their views and preferences are taken into account?

Concluding reflections

Taking a step back and supporting the independence of your students is central to the work of LSAs. Often there is a difficult balance to strike in relation to this, as there is a need to support that independent way of being whilst also ensuring that a student has received enough support to approach their work:

> It all relates back to the dangers of the velcro LSA and the intuition that is required to do this job as you momentarily withdraw yourself from a particular situation whilst also hitting that balance of letting them know that you are available. I think that's a very challenging thing to do.

There are many techniques that LSAs can trial in pursuit of striking this balance – from the check-in method to floating techniques and dual-working approaches. Use your judgement when trialling these methods with your students and be sure to avoid task completion as you support them over the course of your work together: 'At the end of the day, they are the student. They are the learner, and you cannot take away the requirement on them to engage.'

> Consider your own work as an LSA for a moment, in light of this chapter. Might any of these approaches work for you? How might you tweak them to best meet the needs of the students you work with?

References

Bovill, C. (2020) Co-creation in learning and teaching: The case for a whole-class approach in higher education. *High Education 79*, 1023–1037. https://doi.org/10.1007/s10734-019-00453-w

Education & Training Foundation (ETF). (2019). *Learning Support Assistants in Further Education and Training: Guidance for Leaders and Managers*. www.et-foundation.co.uk/document/learning-support-assistants-in-further-education-and-training-guidance-for-leaders-and-managers

Fleming, N. (1995). I'm different; not dumb. Modes of presentation (VARK) in the tertiary classroom, in Zelmer, A, (ed.) *Research and Development in Higher Education, Proceedings of the 1995 Annual Conference of the Higher Education and Research Development Society of Australasia* (HERDSA). HERDSA 18, 308–313. https://vark-learn.com/wp-content/uploads/2014/08/different_not_dumb.pdf

Gerschel, L. (2005). The special educational needs coordinator's role in managing teaching assistants: The Greenwich perspective. *Support for Learning 20*(2), 69–76. https://doi.org/10.1111/j.0268-2141.2005.00364.x

Husmann, P., & O'Loughlin, V. (2019). Another nail in the coffin for learning styles? Disparities among undergraduate anatomy students' study strategies, class performance, and reported VARK learning styles. *Anatomical Sciences Education 12*(1), 6–19. https://doi.org/10.1002/ase.1777

Pauk, W., & Owens, R. (2010). *How to Study in College*. Cengage Learning.

Shor, I. (1992). *Empowering Education: Critical Teaching for Social Change*. University of Chicago Press.

Skipp, A., & Hopwood, V. (2019). *Deployment of Teaching Assistants in Schools: Research Report*. https://assets.publishing.service.gov.uk/media/5d1397fc40f0b6350e1ab56b/Deployment_of_teaching_assistants_report.pdf

University of Staffordshire. (2024, November 29). PEEL Paragraphs: Academic Writing. Library and Learning Services. https://libguides.staffs.ac.uk/academic_writing/PEEL

6
The dialogic LSA

Chapter outline

Chapter 6 examines how LSAs can use dialogue to enrich the educational experiences of their students. I centre the value of dialogue as an educational process, and I reflect on:

- Dialogue vs conversation
- The central role of dialogue in the work of LSAs
- Meeting the student where they are in dialogue
- The richness of the neurodivergent dialogic space
- The creation of fertile dialogic spaces
- Questioning in support of dialogue
- Dialogic pivots
- Dialogue for younger learners

Dialogue vs conversation

Dialogue is intrinsic to the work of LSAs, and indeed to the process of education. People, to a large extent, exist through dialogue (Wittgenstein, 1921). It forms the fabric of our learning and our being. Dialogue is fundamentally different to other forms of conversation (Wegerif, 2020). People can engage in conversations about the weekend and the weather, as these are social interactions that can be largely characterised by social pleasantries (Wegerif, 2020). They are, to an extent, quite predictable and are often underpinned by unwritten 'social scripts' or rules that must be followed to maintain norms and a degree of politeness. Dialogue, however, reflects an essence of education because it is emblematic of a meeting of worlds and a merging of perspectives: true dialogue enables creative thought and the articulation of new ideas, creating the conditions through which people can reach higher planes of understanding and, indeed, being (Kerslake & Wegerif, 2018; Wegerif, 2017a).

I first became interested in dialogue as an undergraduate student, when I attended the lectures of Rupert Wegerif who founded a seminal theory of dialogic education. For Wegerif, there is something deeply transformative and indeed infinite about dialogue as it is a space of infinite possibility – we never truly know where a dialogue may take us, and herein lies a source of rich potential for learning and the development of the self. My experience as an LSA and my own interest in dialogue have shown me that it is an intrinsic part of my work with my students and that dialogue in and of itself can be a desirable goal of LSA working practice.

The role of dialogue in the work of LSAs: why is it important?

Some of my richest learnings as an LSA have occurred through the dialogue I have had with my students. LSAs are in a unique position to approach dialogue and learning conversations with students, as they occupy an educational middle ground between the student and the teacher. They are, moreover, not subject experts: LSAs are often not in a position to provide the right answers or to correct their students. Whilst this lack of subject expertise can be viewed as a disadvantage (and there is, of course, an obvious need for teacher-based instruction in education), I have found that LSAs can encourage wider student learning reflections by encouraging them to 'talk around' their learnings from different subjects, listening to students as they formulate their thoughts and articulate crystallising ideas.

It could even be argued that the fact that the LSA is not a subject teacher is a positive component in support of dialogue: they can help students to reframe ideas and explore different perspectives, safe in the knowledge that the traditional student–teacher hierarchy has been dissolved somewhat. A sense of epistemic humility hence exists within the dialogic space for LSAs: they are aware of their positionality as non-teachers and there isn't a clear-cut expectation for them to guide students academically, as their role is instead to enable a wide variety of students to access their learning. There is thus never an expectation for LSAs to position themselves as an authority within dialogue, and I have found that the LSA dialogic space can be quite fruitful precisely because of this.

The learning conversations, or dialogues, between LSAs and students also reflect the extent to which learning can be positioned as a co-created practice between the LSA and the student, whereby both parties think and reflect together, embarking on a journey collectively to reach higher planes of understanding. LSAs are additionally in a strong position to facilitate forms of 'exploratory talk' with their students where they have the freedom to discuss initial thoughts and seedling ideas in more of an informal and relaxed manner (Barnes, 2008; Wagner, 2015).

Finally, I feel that it is important for LSAs to consider their role in dialogue due to its transformative power to enhance cognition. The ability to engage with dialogue has increasing importance in the world we are living in; socially, we are witnessing a dilution of our ability to engage in effective dialogue with one another, whereby people can cultivate the ability to listen to an opposing view and to consider its nature, without feeling the need to disagree or provide an instant rebuttal. The skills of dialogue are becoming increasingly pivotal for young people, particularly as they engage with a plurality of voices and opinions through mediums such as the internet and omnipresent social media (Wegerif, 2012, 2017b). It is thus, I believe, through a focus on dialogue that LSAs can fulfil an integral extra-curricular function of education, as the facilitation of meaningful dialogue can help to prepare young people for the navigation of an increasingly uncertain world. Indeed, an LSA I interviewed reflected on the importance of dialogue, noting:

> I think [dialogue] is good for socialisation. I think it's very important, especially in the sixth form setting, having your own opinions and being able to develop them on your own as well without our influence and finding appropriate ways to convey them in social settings.

Structuring student dialogues as an LSA: 'You've got to meet the student where they are, rather than where you are'

For one LSA, it was especially important to intentionally make space for students within dialogue, as they articulated their views about the world:

> You're initiating that kind of deeper conversation and you're giving the student a platform to deliver on that more deeply and showing that level of engagement in a way that positions them as the centre and you as the listener – that kind of dynamic certainly has the potential to have a very significant impact.

This LSA and I went on to have an interesting dialogue about dialogue, a snippet of which I will share below to illustrate the importance of listening to your students and not 'over-delivering' when you are supporting them as an LSA:

LSA:

> I think definitely in subjects you specialise in and when the teachers are teaching at a level that is lower than the level that you are familiar with and understand. I think it can be quite easy to get caught up in the arrogance of knowing as much as you do and the tendency to then ramble and over-deliver. That can be a very tempting one but I think it is key to avoid as best you can… You've got to meet the student where they are rather than where you are necessarily.

My response:

> I think I should be mindful of that. Sometimes I can tend to be quite interested in a theme. I've probably done this before, particularly when somebody was studying *Othello*; I think I may have given them a bit of a lecture on the symbolism of the handkerchief. And they don't necessarily need that from me… They can get that from their teacher. I think for me it's about tempering the enthusiasm [within these dialogues] sometimes because I think I'm just interested in what they're doing and I think that's a good quality to have as an LSA. I think to be genuinely interested in that piece of work will bring a level of enthusiasm, which is probably quite positive. I think to really engage with something is good. But for me, I need to not pontificate about stuff because it's probably just not the most helpful. It will probably be better to have more of a dialogue with my students…

The richness of the neurodivergent dialogic space: encouraging special interests and listening to student views

My time as an LSA has impressed upon me the richness of dialogue with my students. Indeed, one LSA I interviewed reflected on their work with their students and noted that 'they are some of the sweetest and funniest and interesting people you will ever meet'. This rings true in my experience. I have learnt so much from my students, and all of this learning has occurred through dialogue, as my students have shared with me their passions for particular interests and their views on political and social issues more broadly.

It has been a privilege of my role to listen to the views of these young people as they articulate their thoughts about the world and their place within it. There is thus immense value, in my view, for LSAs to intentionally create time and space for dialogue with their students. I would suggest marking this as a key priority throughout the course of your work with students, in a manner that suits your time constraints and individual schedule – this might happen during a club or activity, or perhaps during a one-to-one study session or a free period that you may have. Indeed, for one LSA, break and lunchtime duty was a prime time of the day for dialogue with their students:

> We do break and lunch duties. So that's 40 minutes in a room with all the students that particularly don't want to go outside – they might be a bit anxious, or they've just got friend groups that happen to be in that room. You hear some very interesting conversations, and you just instigate dialogue with them; it's actually quite nice to be able to do that because lesson time doesn't necessarily lend itself to that. You get to know those students better and I find that helps in lessons because they may recognise you and they see you as that familiar face.

In sum, remain open to dialogue with your students: embrace the process of dialogue as an educational priority in itself, and try to establish it as a guiding element of your working practice. Remember also not to inadvertently 'close down' learner discussions in classrooms or in academic support departments (Blatchford et al., 2012), in recognition of its rich potential.

When reflecting on dialogue with my students, I have found that some of them have been very keen to speak to me about their special interests and passions. Special interests can be displayed by autistic students, and they often cluster around particular objects or themes that a student finds highly fascinating (Wharmby, 2022). Students with special interests can be very passionate about them, and can often be inclined to share these interests widely with the adults and peers around them. I have found that it is good practice as an LSA to actively engage with students who have special interests, and to listen to them as they discuss their objects or themes of interest. This not only will support students in developing oracy-based skills as they articulate their interests to a broader audience, but it will also help in establishing a supportive educational presence whereby you as an LSA actively engage with the interests and passions of your students.

It can be useful here to remain open to learning from your students in these scenarios, as they can often have insightful knowledge that they are very keen to share. It can be good to show interest by asking follow-up questions surrounding a special area of interest, perhaps by asking a student to expand on why it interests them or by posing questions that encourage them to think more deeply about their object or theme of interest. It is also useful to weave these special interests into academic tasks where possible, perhaps by encouraging your students to examine their special interest in a creative piece of writing or an independent research project (Wharmby, 2022). Students with special interests can thus contribute to an enriched dialogic space, where both LSAs and other students can learn a great deal.

> Consider your own students for a moment. Do they have any particular special interests? How might you bring these interests into a dialogue with them?

Creating fertile spaces for dialogue: warming up the dialogic space and encouraging active listening and humility

Fertile dialogic spaces can often be cultivated in education when participants feel a sense of safety and security when vocalising their thoughts and ideas about the world, some of which may yet to be fully formed (Wagner, 2023). This does not mean they will never be disagreed with or intellectually challenged, but it does require that a level of consideration and respect is utilised when doing so. 'One-upmanship' should be avoided, and it's important that every student has the chance to verbalise their thoughts as part of a dialogue where a plurality of voices are heard and respected:

> We encourage them to have their voices. It's the way that the world is for them. But in order to build that trust, they need to know that you

are listening to them and that you give them time and that they can express how they're feeling or what they think.

I think this is particularly important when working with SEND students, some of whom may have previously experienced forms of epistemic injustice (Fricker, 2007) over the course of their lives, whereby the validity of their knowledge may have been called into question.

In the spirit of creating fertile dialogic spaces, it can be helpful for LSAs to establish themselves as a supportive educational presence for their students, inviting them to bounce their ideas off them or to discuss particular topics of interest. For one LSA, this meant fostering a culture of **openness** whereby students could always come to them to ask questions and to seek clarification:

> I've always said [to students] if you don't know a word or something, or you've heard someone say a word and you don't know if it's bad or not, come to me and I'll tell you. And I won't tell you off.

It is also perhaps useful to consider the individual preferences of students in order to support them in future dialogic participation. Some students could feel uncomfortable participating in public dialogue – for example, if a teacher called on them in class to answer questions or to contribute ideas. Indeed, pupils are highly conscious of how they will be perceived in a classroom setting. An oracy study revealed that secondary school students demonstrated an acute awareness of how their peers might view their in-class contributions (Wagner, 2015). There are, however, some strategies that can help students to feel more comfortable within dialogue. Teachers can use **icebreakers** to help students feel more at ease with in-class contributions – for example, by encouraging them to play verbal ping-pong or to call out the wrong answers to a set question in order to get the dialogic ball rolling in class.

An LSA I interviewed additionally noted that they collaborated well with a teaching colleague to 'get the dialogic ball rolling', as the teacher in question would often lean on them to express initial ideas in class when they encountered periods of silence (and uncertainty) amongst students:

> If no one is going to answer the question, sometimes that class is very quiet and the teacher will look at me and say what do I think? And then I'll go on a tangent and get the ball rolling and it gets the whole class going.

Different technologies could also be explored here to good effect, perhaps by using games such as Kahoot! to enable students to mentally warm up and to organise some initial thoughts and ideas about a topic without having to discuss them publicly in front of their peers.

LSAs also have an important role to play when it comes to encouraging respectful and constructive student dialogue in academic support departments. Although it is important for young people to freely express their thoughts and ideas, LSAs can support them to exchange their views in a constructive manner that is conducive to fruitful dialogue:

> I think we're there to make sure that it stays respectful. There are some times when we have to go 'right, some people might have different opinions and that's OK'. And that's an important lesson for them to learn as well, that you're not going to agree with everybody you meet in life, especially in work life as well. So it's important to know how to still be civil with these people and still get along with them, but you don't have to agree on everything.

In my experience, dialogues that LSAs will hear in academic support departments can often differ from those that will occur in class. Students will often want to discuss extra-curricular themes, such as politics, specific special interests or perhaps recent events that have sparked their interest in a news cycle. These themes offer a rich opportunity for students to engage in constructive dialogue with their peers, in a manner that is perhaps less formal than in-class academic discussions:

> I highly encourage the conversations that happen; I think it builds relationships. It builds friendships that will most likely last. So many friendship groups have formed right in front of us; students have found common interests, whether it's movies, games, history, politics, any of that stuff. It's a very broad room, very diverse. But they're all very respectful, which is the important thing.

It is important, however, to encourage students to **listen** to one another and to avoid talking over their peers. It can thus be constructive for LSAs to encourage turn-taking in student discussions, perhaps by providing students with reminders to listen to the various opinions and views of others, thus ensuring that a plurality of voices have a chance to be heard. I have also personally found it useful to promote a wider culture of humility when students are engaging in such debate and discussion, reminding them that it is important to consider the views of others, without talking over them or feeling the need to 'prove them wrong' or to dominate them intellectually. A sense of humility is indeed integral to fruitful dialogue as it supports the conditions whereby different voices and perspectives can merge in creative tension, without the need for one dominant view to direct (and indeed derail) the dialogue (Wegerif, 2024, 2017a).

Questioning in support of dialogue: providing options and encouraging creative thought

On a practical level, there are a range of questioning strategies that LSAs can employ with students in order to strengthen their approach to dialogue and to enhance pupil engagement and understanding. Questions are highly useful when working as an LSA, as they can be used intentionally to provoke thoughts, generate ideas and boost student engagement with a task. Structured questions that give subtle hints can be particularly helpful for building on student understanding, as they can guide them towards the answer without directly providing it. Questions that feature different options can also be quite helpful for promoting dialogue when discussing certain concepts/words and their meaning. For example, if your student is unsure of the meaning of the word 'forlorn', you could ask them, 'Does that word sound happy or sad to you?' Try to use these questions to prompt your students to think for themselves, and remember not to be too quick to tell them what a word means or what the answer is.

> **Top tip:** Don't be afraid to use student colloquialisms when discussing vocabulary to support a student's understanding – for example, 'an atmosphere is kind of like a *vibe*'.

It's also a good idea to clarify key terms during study sessions and student discussions: do not assume understanding, and check that students are confident with key academic question terms such as 'analyse' and 'evaluate'

The dialogic LSA

before they start their answer. (The same applies to certain concepts as well. I once clarified that my student understood the meaning of the 'political spectrum' during a Sociology one-to-one study session where we were discussing New Labour and Conservative social policies.)

Finally, be mindful of diverse processing speeds when using dialogue with students: don't overload them with too many questions in close succession. Give them ample time and space to reflect on their answer, and prompt them if they seem stuck or unsure ('Would you like me to rephrase the question?').

Reflective questions are also key components for cultivating dialogue with students. Often it is good to frame these questions in response to specific pieces of student work – for example, if your student wrote an Art History essay, you could ask them questions about what inspired them to analyse the work of a certain artist and which aspects of the work held particular resonance with them.

It can also be beneficial to use open-ended and reflective questions within student dialogue, to encourage them to refine their thoughts and ideas when it comes to their studies: 'How might you approach this question?' 'What's your view of this theory?' 'What might a limitation of that concept be?' etc. Keep in mind that dialogues can also be very effective in helping students to appreciate an overarching sense of purpose and utility in relation to their studies. I have found that many different components cluster around a student meeting an A grade, but sometimes it can be beneficial to zoom out of that exam-focused mindset and briefly consider the broader significance of a task. If a student was studying a social theory, for example, you could broaden out the dialogue slightly and ask them, 'What does it mean fundamentally, this theory? What's the essence of this thing? What's the central idea?'

> **Top tip:** When discussing key ideas and concepts, try to get students to verbalise the key idea in a short sentence that is born out of their own words – this can help a lot with clarity of thought and understanding, and it can be useful for them to note their ideas down as a resource to aid future revision.

It can also be useful to ask students why they feel a topic is important and what their opinion on it is: try to encourage them to identify their own critical positionality in relation to key topics. It's important here to emphasise that their opinion matters, and to encourage thoughtful and academically informed critique. This approach may feel as if you are dancing around a topic, but it can help to develop core understandings and depth of thought – I have found that one-to-one study sessions can be a very good space for supporting such thinking.

> **Top tip:** It's important to take an organic interest when discussing student work, and to cultivate an attitude of curiosity and engagement when engaging with students throughout academic dialogue. Try to resist the urge to voice your own thoughts and opinions about their work, and instead cultivate an approach of active listening as they articulate their thoughts and ideas. It is fundamentally important to remain open to learning from students within dialogue as well, in recognition of the fact that they too can provide intriguing ideas and perspectives: 'So it's equal parts me instigating the conversation, but sometimes the students have some really thought provoking and some really interesting pieces of dialogue that are really helpful.' Indeed, another LSA noted: 'The first crucial thing is that it needs to be a dialogue. It needs to be an active conversation between two or more people in order for the student to get the most out of it.'

Finally, remember that dialogue can also be joyful and interesting – its beauty lies in its lack of predictability and stagnation. A colleague of mine was once discussing the future of gaming with a student, and I was struck by the extent to which there was such potential within their dialogue for creative thinking and the generation of new ideas. LSAs have a significant role to play in facilitating a supportive dialogic space, one where young people can be supported in developing new ideas and an enhanced sense of academic self-confidence. In this spirit, have fun with dialogue where it's appropriate and don't hesitate to pose challenging questions to boost student engagement and reflection – sometimes asking 'random' or 'out of the blue' questions ('What if we considered this from a necro-political perspective?') can be useful in regaining student interest and attention:

I think you've got to be a bit eccentric sometimes, I think because if you're just dull and boring, you get what you get – but you have to be a bit 'out there' to make yourself stand out and to make them understand you're there for them.

Dialogic pivots: merging perspectives and encouraging students to hold numerous views in tension

The essence of dialogue clusters around a merging of perspectives, as it concerns the ability of people to engage with different views and perspectives at once, as they effectively hold different voices together in tension (Wegerif, 2017a, 2018). Whilst this operates to a degree at a level of abstraction, I have found over the course of my work as an LSA that I can add small pivots to dialogue, in order to encourage my students to consider the different views and perspectives of their peers more deeply.

I was once having coffee in my academic support department when I overheard two students discussing taxation policies. These two students, from what I could hear, held differing views on fair taxation: one felt that taxes were too high, whilst the other maintained that they were too low. I knew both of these students as I had worked with them before, so I asked them what they thought of the view that taxes could be weighted proportionally based on individual income levels. I was careful to frame this as a question, inviting them to reflect on their own views and positionality in relation to it. It is very important that LSAs do not seek to influence student opinions by inserting their own views into dialogue: this would not be appropriate, nor would it aid the dialogue itself. This small example, however, reflects the extent to which LSAs can add small pivots to dialogue, by posing reflective questions to help students think more deeply about their opinions and views.

I have often thought that it's useful as an LSA to encourage your students to reflect on the architecture of their own knowledge ('How do you know that? Why do you think that's the case?'), as this can help them in fully forming their academic arguments and indeed their ideas about the world. Try to foster an environment of epistemic humility where possible (Wegerif, 2024), encouraging students to respect the opinions of others and to cultivate an attitude of intellectual curiosity where they move away from ideas of 'not knowing' towards a more curiosity-filled stance that embraces the process of learning and the views of others. There are always other positions and different ways of thinking present within dialogue, and part of cultivating a dialogic approach to work as an LSA involves actively inviting students to engage with new perspectives.

> **Top tip:** For dialogic pivots, try to identify the middle ground of the dialogue that students are having at hand (i.e. identify the two core sides of an argument). Once you have distinguished this, ask the students a question that centres around this middle ground ('Have you considered the centrist perspective in relation to this issue?'). Pose this question gently, and encourage your students to reflect on it: remember not to correct one party, or to insert your own opinion into the discussion. Keep in mind that you do not have to be an expert on the topic at hand to encourage students to consider the dialogic 'middle ground' as you are not providing them with clear-cut answers; you are instead posing reflective questions to deepen their thinking and the dialogue itself.

> Consider the dialogues that you commonly have with your students for a moment. What are the themes of interest? What do they like to discuss? How might you utilise such small pivots in dialogue to aid their thoughts and reflections?

Dialogic strategies for younger age groups: clarifying key terms and trialling the think-aloud method

There is also rich potential for dialogue with primary school students. The think-aloud method can be a useful way of fostering dialogue with students from younger age groups and primary school contexts. For one HLTA, this method was particularly useful when paired with text-based discussions – for example, if they were discussing a character or a plot line from a storybook with their students ('I wonder why he did that?'). This HLTA also noted that it was useful to discuss certain themes and ideas from books with students, in support of their engagement and understanding ('I wonder what the word "crimson" might mean?').

For this HLTA, it was particularly important to provide clarity around key words when facilitating dialogue with younger students, particularly concerning terms that may have an unclear or a double meaning such as change, reflection, etc. They also noted that it was important to engage students in dialogue in a fun manner, in order to add a sense of enjoyment to their learning. Often this might involve asking younger pupils for their thoughts and opinions about a story they had recently read or a topic they had recently discussed in class:

> So, in the story the mouse is gazing at the doll's house in the distance. How do you think your facial expressions would be if you were gazing at something? What might your eyes look like, how might your facial expressions change?

A creative and fun approach to dialogue is thus very useful for younger learners, as it can help to facilitate an enriching and joyful learning experience.

Concluding reflections

Dialogue in its true form reflects a meeting of minds and perspectives, opening up new planes of innovation, possibility and understanding as students learn to listen to different voices and to hold conflicting views in tension (Wegerif, 2017a, 2018). My experience in the role has shown me that the work of LSAs is imbued with rich dialogic potential. I believe that helping students to be in dialogue and to become comfortable with dialogic processes will equip them with invaluable skills, as they progress throughout their academic careers and their own lives more broadly. There are, to this end, numerous strategies that LSAs could employ to foster meaningful dialogue with their students as they go about their work in academic support – from dialogic pivots and think-aloud methods, to open-ended questions and reflections on special interests. Although these strategies and methods indicate how dialogue could be approached, it is also worth bearing in mind that there cannot be a pre-packaged, one-size-fits-all approach to dialogue as each one will be inherently unique and unpredictable. I would thus encourage LSAs to embrace dialogue as an overarching process in itself: talk to your students, encourage them to discuss their ideas with each other and with you, and listen to them as they articulate their thoughts and views. Try to enjoy these dialogues as and when they arise - I have found them to be a highlight of my working life, and they are fundamentally worth embracing and dedicating time to.

> Consider your own work with your students for a moment. Does an aspect of this chapter resonate with you particularly? What might a vibrant dialogic space look like in your working context, and what steps could you take to bring it to fruition?

References

Barnes, D. (2008). Exploratory talk for learning. In Mercer, N., & Hodgkinson, S. (eds). *Exploring Talk in School: Inspired by the Work of Douglas Barnes*. SAGE.

Blatchford, P., Russell, A., & Webster, R. (2012). *Reassessing the Impact of Teaching Assistants: How research challenges practice and policy*. Routledge.

Fricker, M. (2007). *Epistemic Injustice: Power and the Ethics of Knowing*. Oxford University Press.

Kerslake, L., & Wegerif, R. (2018). *Theory of Teaching Thinking: International Perspectives*. Routledge.

Wagner, C. (2015). *An investigation into pupil oracy with Year 10 pupils studying GCSE History in an all girls' school*. [Master's dissertation, University of Oxford]. https://ora.ox.ac.uk/objects/uuid:e0ab1adf-4f67-484e-9f8f-048ce2558082

Wagner, C. (2023, June 7). *'Diminished Voices': why is it important to focus on oracy when educating girls?* Oracy Cambridge: The Hughes Hall Centre for Effective Spoken Communication. https://oracycambridge.org/diminished-voices-girls-oracy

Wegerif, R. (2012). *Dialogic Education for the Internet Age*. Routledge.

Wegerif, R. (2017a, September 5). Dialogic space and why we need it. [Rupert Wegerif]. www.rupertwegerif.name/blog/dialogic-space-why-we-need-it

Wegerif, R. (2017b, April 25). 'Post Truth': The Internet, education and democracy. [Rupert Wegerif]. www.rupertwegerif.name/blog/post-truth-the-internet-education-and-democracy

Wegerif, R. (2018, April 29). Dialogue and equality. [Rupert Wegerif]. www.rupertwegerif.name/blog/dialogue-and-equality

Wegerif, R. (2020, February 6). Dialogue Lecture: Languages, Communication and Literacies. [Lecture Notes]. Faculty of Education, University of Cambridge.
Wegerif, R. (2024). Afterword: Dialogic space. *Theory Into Practice 63*(2), 239–250. https://doi.org/10.1080/00405841.2024.2309840
Wharmby, P. (2022, October 14). A personal perspective: How special interests can help autistic students thrive. National Autistic Society. www.autism.org.uk/advice-and-guidance/professional-practice/special-interests
Wittgenstein, L. (1921/2023). *Tractatus Logico-Philosophicus: The New Translation*. Penguin Classics.

7
Assistive technologies for LSAs

Chapter outline

Chapter 7 explores the LSA role as it intersects with assistive technology. I consider:

- LSAs and assistive tech
- Reader pens
- iPads
- MS Teams, email support and shared document editing
- Double screens
- VR headsets
- Microsoft Copilot capabilities
- Support for students with visual learning preferences
- Interdisciplinary learning support
- The value of the human relationship and the need for future training

LSAs and assistive tech: 'I do definitely think we're on the precipice of a dramatically changing educational landscape that the LSA has to be prepared to adapt to'

Technology is catching up with LSAs in education. Many LSAs, at the time of publication, carry out their work in academic support amidst a vibrant technological landscape: students are dialling into classrooms via AV1 robots to overcome barriers to their learning (Fletcher et al., 2024) and generative AI technologies such as Microsoft Copilot are revolutionising the way in which students access information (Weston, 2024). It is in this dynamic context that the work of LSAs could be remade significantly by the proliferation of these assistive technologies across education and learning support:

> Technology is getting better and a lot of the traditional role that an LSM plays is now in a lot of ways better done by technology. When I first came into the career, all my timetable was note-taking in class and reading and scribing in exams. And when I left it, a lot of the reading and scribing was being done by computers and could be done by computers so much more effectively because computers are paying attention. Computers can usually keep up. They don't zone out halfway through a double Maths lesson as I have been known to do sometimes and have to quickly get notes down from a board!

The pace of these technological advances raises, in my view, some important questions for LSAs to reflect on over the course of their work. For one LSA I spoke with, it was important to embrace these advancements with a grain of caution, whilst acknowledging their potential to enhance student learning support:

> I do definitely think we're on the precipice of a dramatically changing educational landscape that the LSA has to be prepared to adapt to with regard to changing technologies, which is I think something that we've got to be particularly cautious around because we're in a kind of eco-system with schools. When I was at university, there was a very strong anti-AI mindset from everyone because of the risks of plagiarism, and that is a risk at this level as well, so it's a matter of supporting the students in a way that empowers them to use new technologies in a way that is helpful and useful to them.

It is also fundamentally important to ensure that students engage with these technologies safely, as recent research has indicated that there is a growing need for comprehensive AI safeguarding frameworks to protect young people from harm and emerging AI 'empathy gaps' (Kurian, 2023a). The rise of AI, moreover, raises intrinsically ethical questions around the nature of education and the value of the human contribution to it: Kurian put it beautifully when she reflected that 'a new device or invention is never simply technical; technology can alter the fabric of society, sway our emotions, and reshape our worldviews' (Kurian, 2023b, p.2).

> Consider your own views for a moment. How do you think the LSA role may be remade in the future given the proliferation of these technologies? What changes might you like to see in this area? How might LSAs harness these technologies for the benefit of their students, whilst safeguarding what remains intrinsically good about their human contribution to education?

Exploring assistive technologies for LSAs

Reader pens

Students often use reader pens throughout their time in education, as they are a key form of literacy support whereby a piece of text is scanned and the words on the page are read aloud. Often, they can form part of official exam access arrangements, with students pairing them with headphones to enable their use in exam halls during assessments.

> **Top tip:** It's important to use these assistive technologies on a regular basis if they are part of a student's official exam access arrangements (Genillard, 2023). Try to incorporate them into one-to-one study sessions and daily class activities as much as possible when working with students, to ensure they are comfortable using them prior to their exams. Many students may also prefer to use reader pens as opposed to having an LSA act as a reader for them in class, and it has significant potential to support an independent approach to studying. Let students trial reader pens if they feel they may benefit, whilst providing initial support to set them up.

Reader pens, in my view, reflect an interesting tension surrounding the reading aspect of the LSA role. LSAs will frequently provide students with a range of support when it comes to reading, often by acting as a reader during exams or by working with a student on a more frequent basis to support with targeted literacy interventions under the direction of a SENCO or a

Assistive technologies for LSAs

specialist teacher. The proliferation of reader pens does, however, raise questions about the future of this practice for LSAs:

> I think reader pens have their place, but also the human element has its place as well. I think when a long question is written in the same tone, it's very easy for students to get distracted or to fall asleep – it will just blur into one for them. Whereas if you're reading it, you'll use different inflexions when you're reading it out, so then it wouldn't be as monotonous.

iPads

In addition to reader pens, iPads can be used by LSAs to enrich their practice and support the learning of their students. They have the advantage of being light and easy to carry, making them a useful tool to utilise in class when working one-to-one with students. For one former LSA, iPads were useful as they featured pencils for digital note-taking, enabling colleagues to share notes across a variety of subjects and classes:

> I quite like using the iPad and I thought it would be a good idea because it meant that you could have all your notes in the same place and everyone could look through different lessons. I think that was the difficulty with A Level subjects: the content can be a bit more complex so when you sit in a lesson and you need to help the student, it can be difficult if you don't really know how to begin because you weren't there for the lesson before. I thought having notes that are ready to share between colleagues would be quite good.

> **Top tip:** If you have an iPad with a digital pencil, it can be a good idea to upload notes on to a central SharePoint or OneDrive system, so colleagues can access them easily to follow up with subject-specific information should they need it.

iPads and PCs also feature a range of useful features for SEND learners, such as speech-to-text dictation software:

Dictation software is fantastic. I know many students who have used it and who loved the way it works for them. I used to work with a student a few years ago and rather than us typing his essays, which could be slow and cumbersome, he would just use the dictate function and then he would have it read back from the computerised voice. The advantage for that, for him, was that he could hear when things weren't right or if he'd misspelt a word. He could hear that voice and [notice when it hadn't been spelt right] whereas me and my colleagues, at the end of the day, we're still human – there are times where we put grammar into our reading because that's the way our brains are programmed to work, so he found that really useful.

I have often encouraged students to try out speech-to-text dictation software during one-to-one study sessions, as it can support them with both essay writing and verbal fluency. It can also be good to use iPads if any students have specific visual requirements, given the usability of its zoom function – encourage your students to use these devices independently where possible, providing set-up support if needed.

> **Top tip:** Utilising speech-to-text dictation software can often be challenging for students in the beginning, as they may initially struggle to think of what to say or could feel self-conscious about verbally expressing their ideas for an essay. Try to support them in verbalising the core of what they want to say, perhaps by working with them to pinpoint the central idea or argument that underpins a paragraph or even an individual sentence. Remind them that the sentence doesn't need to be word-perfect, and that you can always provide them with some light editing help after the initial ideas have been brainstormed. Other students may feel passionately about a particular essay topic, and I have found it can be useful to encourage them to use speech-to-text dictation software when vocalising their ideas and thoughts. Finding the right moment can be key here: you can ask them to 'hold that thought' as you set up speech-to-text, and then you can encourage them to vocalise their ideas once they have pressed the microphone icon to activate the software. Speech-to-text is thus a useful technology that can support students in creating drafts of academic work; it may best be utilised in conjunction with other more traditional methods in order to add variety to a student's study routine.

> Consider your own students for a moment. Have you ever trialled speech-to-text dictation software with them? How did they get on with it? Did they find it helpful when completing their academic tasks?

MS Teams, email support and shared document editing: 'You can see whether they're actually on track or not, without being over their shoulder'

Utilising programs such as Microsoft Teams can additionally enhance LSA support for students. Teams can sometimes work well as a means of 'remote' classroom support, especially if a student prefers working in a manner that is more independently driven in lessons. It can often be good to give students the option of a check-in style form of Teams support (see Chapter 5 for more details), by offering to be available on Teams to answer any questions they may have about their work. LSAs can additionally use Teams to support students to access their learning virtually – they may wish to dial into a lesson via Teams from a safe space, such as an academic support room, with the help of an LSA to set up the Teams meeting and the camera, etc. Trial this option with your students to see if it might work for them – you can also use Teams to check in with students if they are working from home due to factors such as illness. ('The functionality of Microsoft Teams is good. I've had one-to-one sessions with students who have not been in college and who have requested them and that's been very successful so I think there's something to be said for that.')

Finally, Teams can be used by LSAs to generate lesson transcripts for students with hearing requirements (with the teacher's permission, of course!). If you do trial this method of student support in lessons, be sure to factor in extra time to edit the transcript for readability and clarity. It will likely generate quite a chunky block of text, so it is always worth adding things like bullet points, headings, paragraphs and even some colour coding to provide the student with a useful lesson transcript.

For one LSA, it was useful to utilise a form of remote email-based support in class, for a student who did not wish to engage with an LSA over the course of their lesson:

> There was one lad who I was supposed to be in the class with and he absolutely did not want me there. He did not want the LSA to have any contact with him in the room whatsoever, and he's not the only time I've been in that situation. But in his case, what I took to doing was sitting at the back of the room – but I've got a laptop, so I would communicate with him via email in the room. It was a way of letting the lad know that he could ask or give me even just the tiniest nod or just an email back if there was anything he needed without in any way the rest of the class knowing what was going on.

Teams and other forms of digital support such as email can thus be of particular use to students who may wish their LSAs to provide academic support in a discreet manner.

Other LSAs noted that digitally editing documents was a useful way of providing students with essay and work feedback in class, thus reducing the need to physically sit in class with a student if that was against their personal preference:

> I do work digitally sometimes. I'm able to access their work directly so I can see what they're doing, so it doesn't mean I physically sit next to them. I can actually be at the back of the classroom still supporting and directly inputting into a document; I'm accessing the work and making comments. You [could] explain to a student that they need to add more details, I also give them prompts and I normally use a different colour, so they know it's me and that's something we've discussed prior to me doing it actively in their document and I found that quite effective. They can [ultimately reject my suggestion or they can develop on my suggestion].

Indeed, another LSA reflected on their use of a digital educational support program and noted:

> It's an awesome tool, I think one the biggest benefits is the fact that you can interact from afar and you can give compliments, and you can encourage in so many different ways, and you can influence the work that comes out. In the end, you're picking up on little things and I think also the thing that makes it more palatable is that it's constant. You're not just coming back with 'Wouldn't you like to look at these

15 things that you could do differently?' It's a dab in and out, which is really interesting and it's effective because the comments stay visible all the time.

> **Top tip:** Try to keep your comments clear and concise when providing students with feedback digitally. Keep the editing light, and provide spelling, punctuation and sentence structure support. Keep an eye on the individual writing style of the student, and provide them with useful comments to keep their work on track (e.g. you could correct a tense and write a comment such as 'Remember to consistently use the present tense here'). It can also be good to provide prompts and to pose questions, to encourage students to reflect on their argument and to consider their work from a range of theoretical perspectives (e.g. 'Interesting point. How might this link to the feminist perspective on education?'). Remember to check in regularly for digital feedback, and keep in mind that you can always offer students a one-to-one follow-up study session to discuss their work further outside of class in an academic support department.

Double screens

Double screens were identified by an LSA as a useful piece of technology that had strong potential for supporting students with their learning:

> Double screens work really well with the teenagers so that [they have] the information on one screen while they're typing on the other, so they're not having to hold things in their working memory and swap from one task to another, so that's something that we teach them how to use. It's so useful because the children who aren't taught how to split the screen spend a lot of time trying to move it and then sometimes their OCD tendencies kick in and they have to have it exactly the same on both sides. I think it's really useful when it's used correctly to just pop the screen into the right sizing; it's a shame that we don't show more students how to use that more effectively.

The utility of double/split screens resonates strongly with my experience of working with students, as often I have found that some students can spend quite a lot of time navigating various tabs in order to find the key information that they need to progress with their tasks.

> **Top tip:** If it's not possible to access double screens for a student, you can always use the split-screen function of a PC to display multiple tabs or pieces of information on one screen.

There are thus a range of assistive technologies that LSAs can use to support the learning of their students, including reader pens, iPads, Microsoft Teams, digital essay editing software and double screens.

> Consider your work with your own students for a moment. Do you use any of these technologies to support their learning? How might you incorporate assistive technologies into your own practice, to support the needs and preferences of your students?

Virtual reality headsets: supporting students to access higher education and to develop career-based and wider life skills

Virtual reality (VR) software additionally holds vast potential for the support of students, particularly when it comes to helping them to develop career-based and wider life skills. One LSA reflected on their involvement in a VR-based project that was designed to help students develop interview and wider career-based skills:

> The VR project is still in its infancy. I don't think a lot of education settings are using VR to a strong extent yet, but the capacity for it is huge. We have an application on our VR headsets, it's a careers-based application where [students] can train to do anything later in their career setting. So, the student will be given a personalised code, and we'll put them in a room that's VR-ready – there's a lot of space so they

can move around if they want to, or they'll just sit down. And it gives you a bunch of different training courses on different types of careers – so say you're going to do a job interview; you can practise your job interview with the imaginary person in front of you who's not actually there. You'll conduct the interview and you're basically practising, and it will pick out different points of your interview where you said 'umm' and it trains you to conduct yourself in an interview and how to use connecting words instead of saying 'umm'. And there are also other things like behaviour in the workplace, so it's like a little game where you detect where someone's being rude to another person in the workplace, and it will track how many times you press the button and where you've detected it. It's basically this giant course where you can go through it as fast as you want to. It's based around careers support and it's actually in partnership with the careers department in our college.

This LSA also noted the utility of VR when it came to higher education access, as it had the capability of enabling students to access virtual university campus tours:

There's also some students who may not be able to go on trips, say they're not feeling well or they just missed out on the opportunity because of anxiety. There are a lot of universities that do 360 tours now and they are VR-ready, and if they can't go to an open day, for example, they can experience that open day virtually and they can hear people talking about what each area of the university is and where they'll end up working, where they could end up, living accommodation wise, as well.

For another LSA who had experience of using VR, the technology held a lot of potential for the support of students with SEND, noting that it could be further developed in future to help students to refine their travel training skills or navigate their campus:

From the support perspective, we could add to it by helping students who might be anxious about college or maybe even taking a bus into college. You could do a VR [immersion] of taking a bus or even something like if they were going to the cafeteria at lunchtime, they could do it in VR – that might be the first step to them thinking, 'OK, I know the way now and I know what it might be like.'

This idea resonates strongly throughout my own work with students. VR headsets may not work for everyone, but they have interesting potential in providing an element of reassurance for students. It would be interesting to see, for example, how students with sensory preferences might be able to control things like noise levels when riding a virtual bus, as such a VR 'trial run' might help them in taking a first step towards independent travel. VR capabilities thus mark a very interesting area of student support, which LSAs are currently using to enable students to develop important life skills and to overcome certain barriers. It has significant potential for the support of all students, particularly those who may require additional support in developing career-based and wider life skills.

Exploring Copilot capabilities: task chunking and prompt generation for LSAs

Microsoft Copilot is a generative AI software that has rich student support applications (Weston, 2024). I have found that it can be used as a scaffolding support tool for new LSAs or those who are keen to expand their knowledge of scaffolding and task chunking, where pieces of work are broken down into smaller and more manageable components. Copilot can provide support in these areas as it can chunk a task in a matter of seconds, producing useful planning frames or task 'road maps' that LSAs can use to help students with their work.

Follow the steps below to trial Copilot for yourself:

- Open Copilot in your browser and log in with your work account
- Let Copilot know what you need help with by typing an initial message into the 'Message Copilot' chat box (remember to focus only on academic tasks here – never input sensitive student information into any generative AI software)

For example, I used Copilot to generate a planning frame to help me answer a hypothetical Sociology question, where a student had to outline and explain three criticisms of a set theory (e.g. Marxism, Feminism, Functionalism). Copilot generated the image below in response to the following prompt:

> Outline and explain 3 criticisms of (input theory). Can you generate me a simple planning frame to organise my answer? I would like it to be very succinct. It does not need any subject-specific information. I would like something that helps me to think about the link between the criticism and the theory.

This scaffolded task roadmap generated by Copilot could be a good way to structure dialogue around a particular topic with students, helping them to organise their thoughts and to break down a theoretical task into more manageable chunks. I have found it useful when using Copilot to specifically state in the chat box that you do not require a planning frame with subject-specific knowledge. This is key, as you do not want it to generate anything with pre-set answers: use the scaffold/planning frame as a springboard for further discussion and idea generation with your students. When using Copilot or any other form of AI to create resources, remember to always liaise with teachers to ensure that students receive optimal chunked task support. It is also important not to over-rely on Copilot as your sole means of chunking and scaffolding tasks as an LSA, as this is a hugely important pedagogical

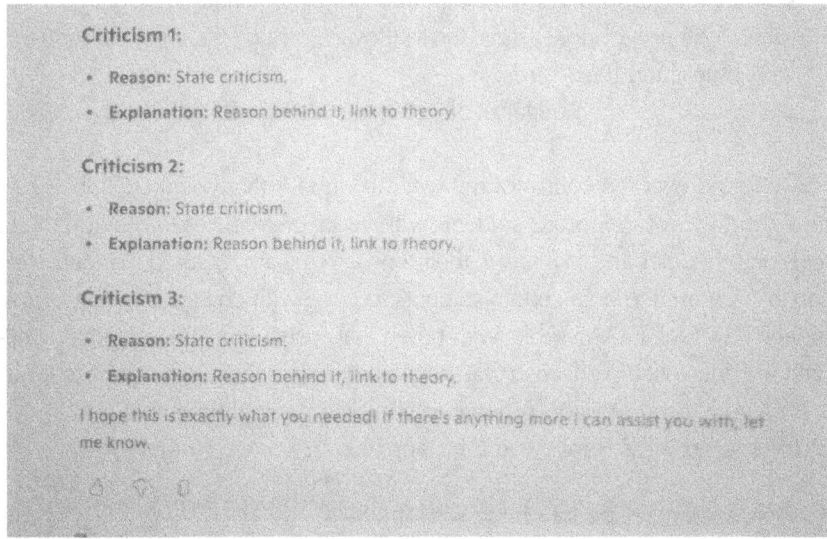

Figure 7.1 A scaffolded roadmap generated by Microsoft Copilot

aspect of your role: use it sparingly, perhaps when in a time crunch or when learning the ropes as a new starter, in a manner that adds value to your work.

Support for students with visual learning preferences

The work of LSAs can often cluster around targeted support for student learning preferences. In practice, this may look like encouraging a student to weave a special interest into a creative writing piece or perhaps compiling something such as a diagram to help them to develop a particular chain of reasoning. The academic utility of supporting individual learning styles has, to an extent, been questioned within educational literature (Husmann & O'Loughlin, 2019). However, Wang et al. (2019) have advocated for a more 'balanced' approach to learning, whereby students receive instruction and support across a range of instructional modes. With the utility of a more balanced approach in mind, there are a range of ways in which LSAs can provide support for students who identify as visual learners:

> Visual learning is defined as the assimilation of information from visual formats. Learners understand information better in the classroom when they see it. Visual information is presented in different formats, such as images, flowcharts, diagrams, video, simulations, graphs, cartoons, colouring books, slide shows/PowerPoint decks, posters, movies, games, and flash cards.
> (Rodger et al., 2009, as cited in Raiyn, 2016, p.115)

I have found over the course of my work as an LSA that visual timetables can be a good way of supporting students with visual preferences to keep on top of revision schedules and to manage their time in a more structured manner. They can also be used to help certain students to cope with change over the course of their day. One HLTA I spoke with noted that 'visual timetables can help children to pencil out their days so that they know how their days are going to look'.

I recently used Copilot software to generate a visual timetable.
In order to do so, I followed the steps below:

- First, I opened Copilot on my web browser
- I then typed my resource requirement into the 'Message Copilot' chat box, using the prompt below:

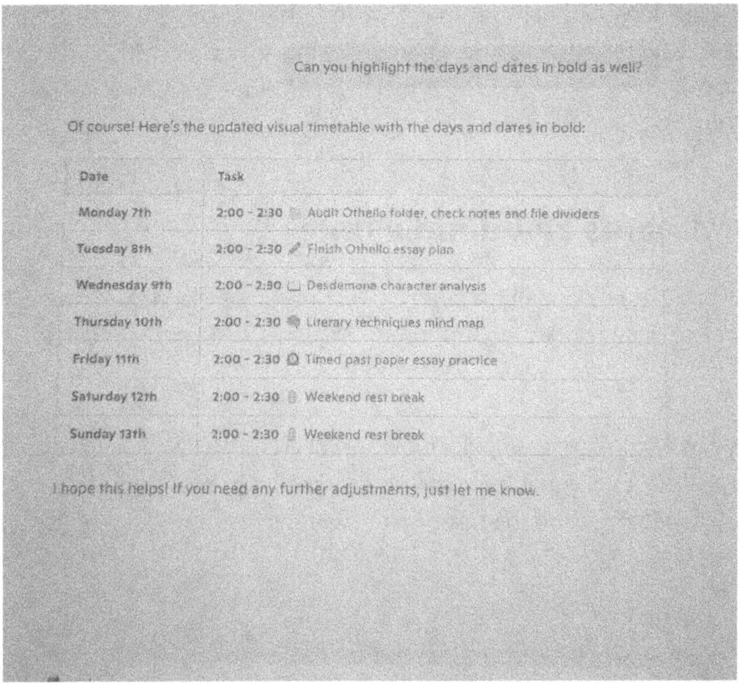

Figure 7.2 A visual timetable generated by Microsoft Copilot

Please can you make me a visual timetable. I need it to have the following **dates**: Monday 7th April until Sunday 13th April. I would like it presented in a **grid**. There need to be 30-minute **work slots**, from 2pm to 2:30pm each day. The following **tasks** need to be included in the timetable: audit Othello folder, check notes and file dividers/finish Othello essay plan/Desdemona character analysis/Literary techniques mind map/Timed past paper essay practice, and then two 'weekend rest break' slots. I would like **emojis/icons** in the timetable – e.g. a green battery for the weekend rest breaks, a folder for the folder audit, pen for the essay plan, timer for the timed past paper, etc.

I have found that it's useful to play around with your Copilot prompts until you are happy with the finished outcome, as I requested that Copilot moved the position of the time stamps and highlighted key dates in bold on my visual timetable. Keep in mind that you can also tailor these resources to best fit the needs of your students – mine was designed to best fit the Easter revision needs of an A Level student, but you could tweak it to reduce the amount of text and to add engaging images if you were making something for a student at primary level. Remember also that these resources are best used when checked over by teachers and when made in partnership with students: work with them to create the resources that will help them, ensuring they are using AI tools safely and productively to add value to their work.

Storyboards and doodle notes

For one HLTA working in the primary school sector, storyboards were a useful tool to draw on when supporting students with preferences for visual learning:

> When we do our writing, I'll draw lots of pictures. I'll get a whiteboard and almost story map out what they're meant to be doing – so say if it was Goldilocks and the three bears, you might draw a little house and then you'll draw Goldilocks.

> **Top tip:** It's a good idea to get students at this level actively involved in the storyboarding process. You could, for example, pose questions to prompt some of their thoughts ('What might happen next?') or you could encourage them to contribute to the storyboard by doing some colouring in ('What colour should the house be?'). For students at higher levels of education, such as secondary school and sixth form, LSAs can utilise mind-mapping software such as Inspiration to support students with visual cues, brainstorming and examining different themes in a manner that is fun and engaging. It is often good to provide demonstrations for students, perhaps with a mind map that relates to a particular theme, to illustrate the utility and functionality of the mind-mapping program.

It can also be fruitful to use images to aid students in their development of descriptive language, as some students may find it easier to describe an object once they have a visual example to refer back to. Google images or generative forms of AI art can also be used to support students with visual

Assistive technologies for LSAs

learning preferences, as they could be used to generate images to support understanding of more abstract concepts. Students may also benefit from accessing things such as graphic novels if they have visual learning preferences. This worked well for one LSA I spoke with who noted:

> For one of my [students], they couldn't access the text, so I got them the graphic novel of the text and that worked really well. They loved that because not only did it have pictures, but it was quite a cool graphic novel.

> **Top tip:** It can be useful to encourage visual learners to add visuals to their revision notes in order to reduce cognitive overload, perhaps by using their own drawings or online tools such as Google images to add an additional layer of engagement to their written materials. This can be particularly useful in content-heavy subjects such as History, Sociology and English Literature. For example, students could add pictures to their notes such as images of key battles and historical figures, pictures of key sociologists such as Émile Durkheim, and even images of key motifs and themes from plays and books, such as a picture of the handkerchief from Shakespeare's *Othello*. Try to encourage students to be creative when writing up their revision notes, and to identify the images that are ultimately of interest to them.

Finally, for one LSA, doodle note-taking was a particularly useful tool for supporting visual learners in class:

> I think doodle note-taking is also really worth exploring. Whilst it's not a technology as such, there are a lot of children who find it really difficult to use technology as well and I think it's an area through art to explore because I think they can make real **visual connections** that sometimes aren't applicable with most of the technologies in use, and I think we could be very quick to disregard the visual impact of traditional mind-mapping and things like that. It takes a different tack, which is very engaging for students and I think it's well worth a look.

My student is a great case in point when she uses it; it makes the information pop out and you highlight different things and it draws in their attention. It's like taking a ball of string and putting the ball of string in the middle and then pulling on the different parts of the string and loosening it until you end up with a web of artistically displayed, well-thought-out ideas. And then you can keep adding and pulling, and that's something that's very difficult to do on the screen when you're using a dictation-type set-up or you're writing. I think it has a different advantage that is hard to replicate elsewhere.

LSAs can thus support students with visual learning preferences through:

- Storyboards
- Mind-mapping software
- Visual timetables
- Google images
- Graphic novels
- Doodle note-taking

> Consider your own work with visual learners for a moment. How do you currently work to support their learning preferences? Might any of these techniques support their studies?

Interdisciplinary learning support: working across the disciplines to support student learning

In addition to VR and AI capabilities, it can be useful to consider the potential of interdisciplinary modes of student support. Interdisciplinary learning concerns the education that occurs through and across academic disciplines and subjects (Corbacho et al., 2021). Essentially, this area looks at the interplay between subjects, and their application when it comes to individual learning support – for example, how might certain scientific ways of thinking help in the study of a subject such as English Literature? This approach to student support is centred fully on the learning preferences of individual students. You may have a student, for example, who demonstrates a preference for clear-cut, logical and highly formulaic modes of thinking – they may favour linear modes of thought, perhaps ones which centre around clear connections between ideas such as a + b = c, no exceptions. In such a case, this student may have a particular aptitude for STEM-based subjects such as Maths or Chemistry. How, however, might an LSA then proceed to support this student when it comes to a subject such as English? In my view, interdisciplinary approaches to support can be useful here, as LSAs could seek to apply the linear cognitive frame of STEM subjects to the study of English. This could perhaps be done by working with students to write up their notes in a formulaic manner during one-to-one study sessions (e.g. quote + evidence = effect).

It is important also to liaise with teachers and to run these ideas by them, to ensure that students receive optimal study support. Keep in mind also that interdisciplinary approaches to learning are best utilised in practice when they align closely with the learning preferences of students. LSAs are, however, often well placed to make observations about the ways in which students learn optimally, due to the proximity of the role and the amount of time spent together in different classes.

> Consider your own students for a moment. What might some of their learning preferences and individual strengths be? Do they relish linear and formulaic modes of thinking, or do they perhaps thrive more on free-flowing dialogue where they can creatively express their thoughts and ideas about their subjects? How might you traverse the disciplines to support their learning in an interdisciplinary manner?

Concluding reflections

LSAs can utilise a range of assistive technologies for the educational advancement of their students, including:

- Reader pens
- iPads
- MS Teams
- Shareable editing documents

- Double screens
- Mind-mapping software
- Copilot
- VR headsets

Many of these have the benefit of saving time for LSAs and providing students with an important sense of independence when engaging with their studies. AI has advanced rapidly in recent years (Weston, 2024), and it is likely that these advancements will continue at pace moving forward, raising some fundamental questions surrounding the work of LSAs as certain core responsibilities of the role could be automated in the future.

Indeed, as one LSA noted when reflecting on this: 'Seriously, a lot of this could be put over to AI. So what can the human do that AI can't? And the answer has to be the human relationship.' This insight perhaps epitomises that whilst certain functions of the LSA role could be outsourced to technology to great effect, there will remain an enduring need for humanising relationships within education. This certainly rang true for one former LSM I spoke with, who reflected:

> I think that we are going to see a bit more of a shift where LSMs and LSAs become a little bit more mental health focused, a little bit closer to that kind of wellbeing realm. So many of our students these days are struggling with anxiety around exams or just life, with everything going on out there, they are struggling with existential depression, struggling with their own mental health, struggling with their own ways of processing the world that is affecting their learning. I think the LSM role will evolve in that direction.

Indeed, another LSA I spoke with remained optimistic about the future of their work in the age of AI:

> I think crucially this is going to be a role that is going to be thriving and still existing and there will still be a high demand for it in the immediate future. With all the kind of panic around AI stealing jobs, even if we do introduce more firmly that kind of technology into the LSA process, you can't remove the human from the app because there needs to be someone facilitating it and there needs to be someone guiding

the students through that so they have the platform to maximise the whole situation for themselves. I think with that in mind, this definitely is going to be a role that's going to be thriving down the line.

The rise of these technologies also indicates a core need for future LSA training support ('I think there will be an aspect where LSAs need to become more technologically aware'), so they can access reliable information and guidance that will enable them to harness these technologies optimally – and safely – for the benefit of students:

> I think also with developing technologies, with the kind of world that we're living in, especially with regard to AI, that potentially some training in that area could be useful to LSAs who are sort of coming up. That could definitely be helpful to have somewhere down the line... It's a matter of supporting the students in a way that empowers them to use new technologies in a way that is helpful and useful to them. (And I think that's probably the most important reason why specialist training in this area will probably be required for anyone who's working in a school because the mindset of generative AI being only good for plagiarism, I don't think it's helpful for anyone operating at any level in the education system.)

I would encourage LSAs in the field at present to remember that this technology is likely to change and advance at pace over the course of their time in the role. We are working in a shifting technological landscape, so don't hesitate to seek out information and support when it comes to your use of these technologies: there are many options available – indeed, this chapter has considered but a few – and a great number of them can be of value and utility when it comes to student support and time efficiency. Stay curious and proceed with safety and a grain of caution as you test out the tech that might work for you and your students. Be wary of the extent to which AI might be used to do the pedagogical work for you and never forget the value of the inherently human contribution that you make each day to support young people. I hope this chapter may offer some points of reflection for LSAs in the field, particularly those who have an interest in the potential for assistive technology to support student outcomes.

> Consider your work as an LSA for a moment, with the insights of this chapter in mind. What do you think the LSA role will look like in 50 years, given the rapid technological advancements that are currently shaping the educational sector? What kind of training might help you in this area, and how might you optimally utilise assistive technologies to support the learning of your own students?

References

Corbacho, A, M., Minini, L., Pereyra, M., Gonzalez-Fernandez, A, E., Echaniz, R., Repetto, L., Cruz, P., Fernandez-Damonte, V., Lorieto, A., & Basile, M. (2021). Interdisciplinary higher education with a focus on academic motivation and teamwork diversity. *International Journal of Educational Research 2*(2021), 100062. https://doi.org/10.1016/j.ijedro.2021.100062

Fletcher, M., Bond, C., & Qualter, P. (2024). Using AV1 robots to support pupils with physical and emotional health needs. *Educational Psychology in Practice 40*(1), 74–95. https://doi.org/10.1080/02667363.2023.2269082

Genillard, T. (2023, January 24). Preparing students with access arrangements for exam success in social science subjects. OCR Oxford Cambridge and RSA. www.ocr.org.uk/blog/preparing-students-with-access-arrangements-for-exam-success-social-science

Husmann, P., & O'Loughlin, V. (2019). Another nail in the coffin for learning styles? disparities among undergraduate anatomy students' study strategies, class performance, and reported VARK learning styles. *Anatomical Sciences Education 12*(1), 6–19. https://doi.org/10.1002/ase.1777

Kurian, N. (2023a). AI's empathy gap: The risks of conversational Artificial Intelligence for young children's well-being and key ethical considerations for early childhood education and care. *Contemporary Issues in Early Childhood*. https://doi.org/10.1177/14639491231206004

Kurian, N. (2023b). Toddlers and robots? The ethics of supporting young children with disabilities with AI companions and the implications for children's rights. *International Journal of Human Rights Education 7*(1). https://repository.usfca.edu/ijhre/vol7/iss1/9

Raiyn, J. (2016). The role of visual learning in improving students' high-order thinking skills. *Journal of Education and Practice 7*(24). www.iiste.org/Journals/index.php/JEP/article/view/32607

Rodger, S, H., Qin, H., Hayes, J., Nelson, D., Lezin, G., & Tucker, R. (2009). Engaging Middle School Teachers and Students with Alice in a Diverse Set of Subjects. *SIGCSE '09: Proceedings of the 40th ACM technical symposium on computer science education*. https://doi.org/10.1145/1508865.1508967

Wang, J., Mendori, T., & Hoel, T. (2019). Strategies for multimedia learning object recommendation in a language learning support system: Verbal learners vs. visual learners. *International Journal of Human–Computer Interaction 35*(4–5), 345–355, https://doi.org/10.1080/10447318.2018.1543085

Weston, A. (2024). *Empowering Young Minds: AI Conversations and Visuals Custom-Fit for Every Student.* Long Road Sixth Form College, Cambridge.

8
Looking to the future: redefining the LSA?

Chapter outline

Chapter 8 looks to the future, as I examine potential changes to the work of LSAs in education. I consider:

- The LSA training landscape
- LSA training goals: from scaffolding support to future investment
- LSA training opportunities: current knowledge gaps and an LSA qualification?
- Training on the job as an LSA: mentoring and shadowing opportunities
- The lived LSA knowledge base in education
- Future LSA pay reform
- Greater understanding and appreciation
- Day-to-day working improvements for LSAs
- A view to the future: where might we go from here (and why does it matter)?

The LSA training landscape: 'I think new people come in, and a lot of it is finding their feet and just learning on the job'

Training underpins an integral aspect of LSAs' ability to support students and to work optimally within education (Breyer et al., 2021). Students in a post-pandemic educational landscape are facing increasingly complex challenges (Adams, 2024; Major et al., 2024; Cattan et al., 2023), and it is vital that well-trained and highly motivated LSAs are equipped to meet their needs effectively ('I think there are gaps in knowledge; we have a very high number of autistic children here and I think the understanding really varies between colleagues depending on what they have done before').

LSAs operate in a largely pick-and-mix training landscape: 'most LSAs do not have to complete a specific training programme for supporting students with SEN in their learning' (Breyer et al., 2021, p.349), and although some EHC plans can stipulate certain support staff training recommendations, it often falls to individual departments and schools to provide LSAs with training (ETF, 2019).

For many of the LSAs I interviewed, there was clear scope for future improvement when it came to their training:

> There have definitely been times when I've been working with students and I have thought 'Should I have had specialist training around how to deal with this situation?' It definitely took me a while to learn how the best way to plan ahead was so I was not having to do as much thinking on my feet. I think a little more grounded support in that area could do the world of good in that early stage.

This can be especially true when it comes to the early days of working as an LSA: 'I think new people come in, and a lot of it is finding their feet and just learning on the job.'

LSA training goals: scaffolding, challenging higher-ability students, future investment and barriers to training

For one learning coach I spoke with, it was important for newcomer LSAs to receive SEND terminology training in the early days of their practice, as many can enter the profession with limited SEND experience: 'You've probably heard of autism, but you might not know anything about it or how it presents or the background to it. You might not have any idea what someone means by sensory needs.'

Specific **scaffolding** support was noted as a future training improvement for one LSA, who reflected:

> I think training in how to successfully scaffold work without doing it yourself would be helpful. It can be tricky to get the balance right

with knowing how to scaffold a piece of work for students so that they can access it for themselves – because it's all too easy to just slip into doing the work for them.

Access to a balance of in-person and **online** training opportunities was a priority for some:

> A lot of the training that you have is online, and I wish we'd have more training that was face to face. I enjoy online training for some things, but personally, if I'm staring at a screen for long periods of time, I'll just zone out and things don't go in my head. Whereas if someone is speaking to me face to face, if it's a conversation, I learn so much quicker and I retain so much more because I remember specific moments. So I think that the training we have is great, but maybe a face-to-face, in-person version of that same thing would be even better.

One HLTA also noted that they would like to receive guidance on how to effectively **challenge higher-ability students** in class, to enable the teacher to focus more on students with additional needs:

> If you put your LSA with your really higher-attaining students, then they've got the chance to really push those children and let them flourish, so I think training about how you can push those higher-attaining students would be really helpful. I think that's almost like a gap in the market where actually if your teacher works with those students, they can give them lots of extra support and the teacher also knows where they are in class.

Some LSAs, however, noted that **access to training** was a challenge in itself: 'It's less about what training is going to be useful and more about when are they going to have the time to do it.' A core future improvement to the work of LSAs thus lies in improved access to expertise and professional SEND knowledge, in support of both their CPD and their daily work with students:

> We should [have] have specialists come in and talk about different things, like what is autism or what is ADHD and how can we support children. We should have outside specialists in, like speech and language specialists

and OTs and physios to provide training sessions so that you have a more rounded view of the children that you're working with.

Granting LSAs dedicated time to complete this training is a further priority in my view, as LSAs with gaps in their knowledge and a lack of time to dedicate to training may struggle to provide the most effective support to students with complex needs. One LSA noted that future investment was needed when it came to LSA training:

> I think **investment** in CPD for LSAs would be brilliant. But I think schools need to really invest in providing training for LSAs to make sure that when they start in a new school, they're not just thrown into it and told 'right, go and work with these kids'.

There are thus significant future improvements to be made to the LSA training landscape, including:

- Scaffolding training
- In-person and online training opportunities
- Training to support higher-ability students
- Access to SEND knowledge and dedicated training time
- Future investment

Consider your own training needs for a moment. What training might benefit your work with your current students? How might you be supported to meet your future training goals?

Top tip: Take ownership of your training needs as an LSA: don't hesitate to communicate with your manager or SENCO if you feel there is an area in which you would benefit from further training. Make sure to keep a note of your training requests, so there is a record that you sought out additional CPD opportunities in order to support your students effectively.

LSA training opportunities: current knowledge gaps and a future qualification?

The current fragmentation of the LSA training landscape raises fundamental questions about what changes are needed in order to address key LSA knowledge gaps:

> A couple of things have cropped up this year. I've ended up working one to one with a student and we thought there was a dyslexia issue, and I've not had any training in working with people with dyslexia. But you're expected to sort of [do it anyway]. But how am I supposed to know these things if I've not had any training?'

One potential training reform may lie in a more formalised qualification framework for LSAs.

Access to an LSA-based training qualification could, in my view, solve a number of issues that currently cluster around the LSA working landscape ('At the moment it is an unqualified role. And it really shouldn't be'). Access to such a programme could support LSAs in developing a detailed SEND knowledge base to enhance the support that they provide to their students. Certain core modules (such as ones examining autism, social, emotional and mental health (SEMH), ADHD, anxiety, dyslexia, visual impairment (VI) and hearing support) could be compulsory, with further opportunities to pick and mix optional modules to best meet the needs of specific students. It would be brilliant if successful completion of such a course could be coupled with bespoke career development opportunities for LSAs: it could be marked as an entry-level requirement for an assistant SENCO role for example, enabling LSAs to deepen their SEND knowledge base in a manner that would support future career progression:

> As an LSA, there isn't as much progression unless you want to be a teacher, which isn't really a career that I wanted. I really did enjoy working [as an LSA] because I felt like the work was very meaningful, but I think it was time to move on. It'd be nice for an LSA to have more progression routes, because there's a lot of roles in education and you don't have to always become a teacher.

Supporting access to such a qualification would also, in my mind, bring a much-needed professionalisation to the LSA role, whilst signifying a wider investment in SEND and the work of LSAs more broadly. It would need to be fully funded on a practical level, and it would be important for LSAs to receive dedicated training time throughout their working week, perhaps timetabled in a similar vein as teacher planning, preparation and assessment (PPA) time. Whilst such a programme would undoubtedly require significant resources to implement, it would arguably be an investment worth making in support of SEND educational outcomes. Such reform is of particular importance as of late, as a recent NAO report indicated that the current system of SEND provision is ceasing to be fit for purpose (NAO, 2024). Change of some kind is thus required imminently, and this is perhaps a timely moment for LSAs in the field to reflect on the future changes that they would like to see in relation to their training and career development opportunities.

> Consider your own views on LSA training for a moment. Have you completed any SEND training courses? What changes would you like to see to LSA training opportunities in the future?

Training on the job: departmental mentoring and shadowing opportunities

For many LSAs, training on the job at a departmental level additionally underpinned a core aspect of their preparedness for the role. **Shadowing** was particularly important for some new starters, as it enabled them to observe support interventions in real time and to ask any questions that came to mind. Shadowing also has the benefit of enabling new starters to observe a range of different LSA support strategies, broadening their knowledge base and giving them insightful real-time exposure to different ways of working as an LSA:

> I'll model the intervention to the LSA. Say it was a phonics one, I would let them sit in and watch me do the intervention and then together we would kind of team-teach it. That was really effective for

those new members of staff because then they had that opportunity to ask a question as they were going along.

> **Top tip:** There is often a wealth of knowledge within academic support departments, and it can be a good idea to do a skills audit of your team. Identify key areas of expertise (dyslexia, SEMH, autism spectrum condition, ADHD, visual/hearing impairments, etc) and liaise with colleagues to enquire about shadowing opportunities and extra resources if you think this may be beneficial:
>
> It would be useful to actually see a specialist teacher [do a support intervention] and use the skills that we would also use with students. It creates a visual, almost like a script of how to handle a situation, if it comes up.
>
> Remember to gain student consent prior to shadowing one-to-one sessions, ensure they are on board with your presence, and remember to discuss new starter shadowing in advance with students who may be particularly sensitive to change.

For one HLTA I spoke with, inter-departmental **mentoring** opportunities were important for new starters, as it provided them with a key point of contact to discuss queries and concerns: 'Having a mentoring system for LSAs who are brand new will be really helpful because then you've got someone who you can rely on and you've got someone who can show you what you need to be doing.' Training as an LSA and settling into the job in the early days of your role can also be quite **overwhelming**. This was the case for one LSA I spoke with, who reflected on the huge training load when it came to areas such as SEND and safeguarding: 'I look at how our new LSAs are probably feeling, which is overwhelmed with the sheer number of things that they need to catch up with.'

> **Top tip:** Always reach out to your mentor, colleagues, SENCO or line manager if you are feeling overwhelmed in the early stages of your role. There is a lot to get to grips and it's important to ask for help if you

need it (see Chapter 2 for tips on protecting your own wellbeing as an LSA). Try to check in with your mentor regularly in the beginning, to ensure you are on the same page as you get to know your new students and teaching colleagues. It's also a good idea to speak to your manager if you are feeling overwhelmed with your training requirements: ask them if you can pencil some training slots into your calendar to help you get up to date.

Consider your own introductory training as an LSA for a moment. What training did you receive? Did you shadow colleagues, or work with a mentor? What might a strong programme of introductory training have looked like, in your view?

Bridging the gap between theory and practice – the lived LSA knowledge base: 'That's when your practice stops being "this is what the book says" and starts being "this is what helps"'

Whilst training is an integral aspect of strong LSA support, practical application is just as important:

> You can learn so much from a book that will teach you about teaching and education and learning support. They're brilliant, there are these wonderful theories… but until you start having those conversations [with students] and going, 'Right, so we've been trying this for three weeks, how's that working for you? Oh, that you found X really helpful, so what if we tried introducing it over here?' That's when your practice stops being 'this is what the book says' and starts being 'this is what helps'.

LSAs, in many ways, make their own knowledge within education, as they support students with increasingly complex needs to access their learning:

> We facilitate all sorts of help on the physical side, as well as the academic and mental health sides. We have different students who need different types of support, so really we need to adjust ourselves to each individual need.

Often this lived LSA knowledge base will stem from the one-to-one proximity of the role: LSAs work closely with their students each day, getting to know them and building supportive educational relationships where they slowly, over time, will learn 'what works' and what doesn't. I believe there is immense value in this form of grounded LSA knowledge: access to accredited training, of course, remains essential for optimal student support, but there remains a lot to be said for the rich lived SEND support experience that LSAs bring to their work each day.

This grounded SEND knowledge base emerged over time for one participant I spoke with, who reflected on an instance where they supported a student with dissociation to access their learning:

> They would just sort of entirely disconnect. And I would just try things, I would sit there and mundanely chat about my day or tell awful, awful jokes, whatever kind of happened to cross my mind, and over time we sort of built this kind of road map of, like, we don't know what pushes her into it, we don't really know what brings her out of it, but we know that these things help and these are some tactics to go with.

Whilst it remains imperative to adhere to professional guidance when working with students with complex needs, there is also scope for LSAs and their educational colleagues to work closely with students on the ground as they navigate the complex terrain of establishing what might work to support them on a day-to-day basis.

> Consider your own work as an LSA for a moment. Have you ever 'made your own knowledge' when supporting a student? Think of your specific support strategies here, and the extent to which you might make small tweaks to your support to best meet the needs of your students.

> **Top tip:** It is quite useful to adopt a student-centred approach to training and CPD. Every student will present differently, and the key to effective practice lies in your ability to apply foundational SEND principles to individual situations. Keep in mind also that some students may ultimately present in unique ways that you have not necessarily been trained to respond to. Try to be patient in these situations: get to know the student and lean on experienced colleagues for support, as you spend time learning how best to support them in practice. Slowly, over time, you will begin to identify some effective support strategies. Try to keep a secure record of successful support interventions, to help you to track patterns and identify points of strong practice. Don't hesitate to share your knowledge as and when you craft it: there is often a lot to learn from LSA colleagues who may embrace modes of student support that are entirely different from your own but just as effective in their own way.

Future LSA pay reform

In the spirit of looking to the future, the LSAs I spoke with reflected on a number of changes to their working lives when it came to:

- Pay reform
- Greater recognition
- Day-to-day work improvements

For the vast majority of LSAs I interviewed, **pay** was a significant aspect of their work that required improvement:

> I mean it's horrible to say, but money is the thing because if [students] aren't getting the help they need, the situation is getting worse and the job is getting more stressful, and people are starting to leave. And then it's just not as appealing as a job because people are saying, oh, actually I can leave and go and work at Costa and earn more and it's less stressful.

Indeed, one LSA reflected that making ends meet on their salary was particularly challenging as they lived in an area with a high cost of living and were financially compelled to offer extra tuition classes outside of school hours to make ends meet ('We don't have high salaries and we do extra work as well, extra tutoring'). Many LSAs I have worked with have needed to take on additional weekend and summertime jobs and 'side hustles' in order to boost their income outside of term time.

For one former LSA, the issue of future pay reform was particularly important as they didn't feel that their salary aligned with the high levels of **responsibility** that came with their role:

> It's not a nine-to-five office job. Every day is different and every day can be difficult: you can deal with people that are really happy to see you one day and then the next day, they don't want to see you, and it's the emotional toll, the amount of kind of preparation that goes into it, and it's not something where you just wake up and you pop into work: you've got to go in with a game plan. And I don't think that's fairly reflected in terms of LSA pay.

Low pay was identified as an issue by one former LSA I spoke with, particularly in light of recent **cost-of-living** increases:

> It's quite a hard salary to live on and I'm sure teaching assistants feel that way and teachers themselves as well. I think better pay would be good. Teaching assistants and support staff play quite a central role in education, and teachers do a wonderful job, but they have their limits. It's quite important to have support staff because, especially at the moment when students with EHCPs are rising, we need more support, and we need to encourage more people into the role. I think it's mostly just that because I think as support staff as well, you might be roped into other things, so you do end up doing quite a lot for students, and it should be reflected in the pay. And that's the whole point about education in general for teachers as well – they're not getting paid enough for the amount of work that they do, and education is a very important part of society.

Issues with low pay for LSA and educational support staff have intensified in recent years due to ongoing cost-of-living pressures, with many gravitating towards the retail sector in search of higher salaries and full-time contracts (Topping, 2022). A starting point for future improvement would thus be a revision of LSA pay scales; an annual salary of £25,000 would, in my view, be a more reasonable remuneration for the hard work and valuable skillsets that many LSAs bring to the role (Ion, 2024). Full-Time Equivalent pay scales should also be revised, in recognition of the fact that many LSAs require paid holidays in order to avoid burnout and the associated higher rates of sick leave and work absence (Kinman et al., 2011; Savage, 2022). I also would like to see LSA contract improvements: LSAs should enjoy permanent job security, and their salaries should increase incrementally, in recognition of greater LSA experience and enhanced skillsets:

> The structure for LSAs is very flat so in teaching you can become a head of department, and you can get more responsibilities and a higher salary. But with an LSA, you can work in the role for ten years and still be paid pretty much the same as somebody who's just come in with maybe 18 months' experience just because the structure is so flat.

Consider your own views on LSA pay scales for a moment. What improvements would you like to see in this area?

Greater understanding and appreciation: 'I think the cultural attitude of the institutions could change. Nobody is anti-LSAs, but I think an awful lot more could be said in their favour'

In addition to pay improvements, there is a need for change on a cultural level through greater appreciation of the work that LSAs do within education: 'So I think it would be really nice if there was just more **value** towards the LSA role.' This was especially important for one learning coach I spoke with, who reflected on the importance of receiving positive recognition for their work from the upper echelons within their own institution:

> We're really lucky that our senior leader is so supportive. Every time we have a meeting, she says this school wouldn't run without you,

> you are the heart and soul of the team. So the actual wording of how people talk about us and actually being acknowledged, that makes a massive difference from the SLT and I think the head and the team have learnt from her and so the school has that kind of **ethos** which I think is really positive.

In addition to greater appreciation, there is also a need for the role to be understood and appreciated in its entirety:

> I think that in a bigger picture sense, normalising it and actually **broadening the understandings of what LSAs are for** [is essential] because I think if you look in the future in 10/15 years, you would probably think 'wow there were not enough LSAs'.

The importance of a deeper understanding of the work of LSAs resonates strongly with my experience of the role. LSAs can sometimes be seen as general 'support workers' or note-takers and prompters in lessons – and whilst these are aspects of the role, its scope is collectively much broader than that:

> I think there needs to be more crossover, more education to show the way of thinking [that underpins the LSA role]... so why do you need it printed on different piece of paper? Or why would you bother doing that? I think there is a lack of education about why you're doing what you do, and that devalues the role of the LSA in the room. And I think it's really important that these things are shared, so people can actually understand the value of the work.

Day-to-day working improvements: enhanced autonomy, dedicated prep time and fuller utilisation in class

In addition to improved pay and a stronger appreciation for their work, LSAs noted a range of future improvements that would enhance their working lives on a day-to-day basis. For one LSA, this clustered around greater **autonomy** to structure their time over the course of their working day. For them, it was essential that they were trusted to make key decisions in their work, particularly when it came to student support and when it was appropriate to 'take a step back' to allow a student to work independently for a chunk of time:

> We are professional enough to know our students well enough to say, 'I know what they're like in this lesson. They're typically going to get on OK, let's leave them to it.' Or I'm going to go and check in on them for the first five minutes, then let them crack on. LSAs are professionals and they know what they are doing.

On a day-to-day basis, there are additionally a range of improvements that would enhance the work of LSAs: I think LSAs should be given dedicated admin, training and preparation time – timetabled, in a similar vein to teacher PPA time – in order both to address workload issues and to enhance their support for students. LSAs with a lack of time to prepare resources and support strategies will ultimately struggle to provide the most effective support for students, and it is important that investments are made in these areas in the interests of good working practice.

Additional changes could also perhaps be made to attract graduates to the profession, such as certain working-from-home opportunities in order to enable LSAs to effectively pursue training opportunities and key research and planning tasks (Teach First, 2024).

Finally, one LSA noted that the role could be improved in the future through optimal in-class utilisation: 'I think that perhaps [the focus should be taken away from] some of those jobs that are a little bit mundane. LSAs should be used to their fullest in every sense.' This was echoed by another participant, who noted the importance of drawing on LSA skills to the fullest educational extent: 'We've got a lot of Spanish TAs; why aren't they being asked to come in and help with a Spanish lesson?'

> **Top teacher tip:** A full utilisation of LSAs in class clusters largely around a degree of active involvement: LSAs should feel a sense of belonging in the classroom, and this can be achieved by strategies such as teacher-directed in-class floating techniques (see Chapter 5 for more detail).

> Consider your own work as an LSA for a moment. What future improvements would you like to see to the role? What small tweaks might support your day-to-day tasks?

Concluding reflections

I think it's fair to say that LSAs are facing something of a critical juncture at present. Many are leaving the profession in search of permanent contracts and higher salaries (Fazackerley, 2023; Unison, 2022), whilst those who remain are working within a system of SEND support that is ceasing to be fit for purpose (NAO, 2024). Future reform is needed in order to stem these issues, and it is my view that SEND students should be supported throughout their education by consistent and highly trained LSAs who are valued for the work they do and who are incentivised to stay in their roles through a system of adequate recompense.

There are, perhaps, reasons to remain hopeful for some future change as the current government recently delivered on their manifesto commitment to reinstate the SSSNB: 'School support staff play a vital role in children's education and development. Labour will reinstate the School Support Staff Negotiating Body, which will help address the acute recruitment and retention crisis in support roles' (Labour, 2024; DfE, 2024). Many questions remain, however, about how best to solve these issues – ones which should be pondered by both LSAs and those at the highest levels of SEND support provision. My ultimate hope is that the views of LSAs will lie at the heart of any future reform that shapes their working lives, as they chart a future path towards inclusive educational provision for all.

> Consider your own views for a moment. How do you think the LSA role could be improved moving forward? What future changes would you like to see, and what steps might you take to bring them to fruition?

References

Adams, R. (2024, August 25). 'Bubble' of post-pandemic bad behaviour among pupils predicted to peak. *The Guardian*. www.theguardian.com/education/article/2024/aug/25/bubble-of-post-pandemic-bad-behaviour-among-pupils-predicted-to-peak

Breyer, C., Lederer, J., & Gasteiger-Klicpera, B. (2021) Learning and support assistants in inclusive education: A transnational analysis of assistance services in Europe. *European Journal of Special Needs Education* 36(3), 344–357. https://doi.org/10.1080/08856257.2020.1754546

Cattan, S., Farquharson, C., Krutikova, S., McKendrick, A., & Sevilla, A. (2023, August 1). Almost half of children saw their social and emotional skills worsen during the pandemic – and economic turbulence played a role. Institute for Fiscal Studies. https://ifs.org.uk/news/almost-half-children-saw-their-social-and-emotional-skills-worsen-during-pandemic-and-economic

DfE. (2024). School support staff body reinstated: The School Support Staff Negotiating Body will ensure school support staff are valued and recognised for the vital work they do. www.gov.uk/government/news/school-support-staff-body-reinstated

Education & Training Foundation (ETF). (2019). *Learning Support Assistants in Further Education and Training: Guidance for Leaders and Managers*. www.et-foundation.co.uk/document/learning-support-assistants-in-further-education-and-training-guidance-for-leaders-and-managers

Fazackerley, A. (2023, May 14). Low pay 'forcing teaching assistants out of UK classrooms'. *The Guardian*. www.theguardian.com/education/2023/may/14/low-pay-teaching-assistants-uk-classrooms

Ion, M. (2024, February 7). Labour should rebrand TA job title and boost pay to £25k. *TES Magazine*. www.tes.com/magazine/analysis/general/labour-teaching-assistants-boost-pay-recruitment-retention

Kinman, G., Wray, S., & Strange, C. (2011). Emotional labour, burnout and job satisfaction in UK teachers: The role of workplace social support. *Educational Psychology* 31(7), 843–856. https://doi.org/10.1080/01443410.2011.608650

Labour. (2024). Break down barriers to opportunity. https://labour.org.uk/change/break-down-barriers-to-opportunity

Major, L. E., Eyles, A., Lillywhite, E., & Machin, S. (2024). *A generation at risk: Rebalancing education in the post-pandemic era*. www.nuffieldfoundation.org/wp-content/uploads/2022/02/A-generation-at-risk-rebalancing-education-in-the-post-pandemic-era-1.pdf

National Audit Office. (2024). *Support for children and young people with special educational needs*. www.nao.org.uk/reports/support-for-children-and-young-people-with-special-educational-needs/#conclusions

Savage, M. (2022, July 31). Teacher sick days soar as poor conditions take toll on mental health. *The Guardian*. www.theguardian.com/education/2022/jul/31/teacher-sick-days-soar-as-poor-conditions-take-toll-on-mental-health

Teach First. (2024). *Tomorrow's teachers: A roadmap to get Gen Z into the classroom*. www.teachfirst.org.uk/reports/tomorrows-teachers

Topping, A. (2022, September 8). Schools in England risk losing TAs to supermarkets over 'chronic' low pay. *The Guardian*. www.theguardian.com/education/2022/sep/08/schools-risk-losing-teaching-assistants-to-supermarkets-chronic-low-pay-report

Unison. (2022). School support staff cost-of-living survey 2022. www.unison.org.uk/content/uploads/2022/11/UNISON-survey-for-Stars-22.pdf

Conclusion

Whilst few things in life are without their challenges, writing this book has been a labour of love for me over this past year. I have enjoyed connecting with LSAs from various educational backgrounds who have generously shared their reflections and experiences with me in support of this work. Our discussions have helped me to refine my own working practice, and I have been hugely inspired by the work that they do in support of their students: 'Learning support mentors are a school's humanity and if everyone else is doing their job, then a learning support mentor just caring about the individuals makes everything flow.' This book belongs not just to me, but to all who have contributed to it: it is an amalgamation of their voices, perspectives and ideas.

I have sought over the course of this work to offer some insights and reflective questions, as opposed to clear-cut answers. I felt this was important because the work of LSAs doesn't necessarily operate like that in my experience: LSAs exist in their own eco-system, shaped by student needs and the relationships they build with them. What works for one LSA may not work for another: there can be no guidebook, nor a one-size-fits-all approach to the work of LSAs, and I intended to structure this book in a manner that reflects that.

Writing this book has indeed felt like a dialogue in many ways: I have danced with the voices and insights of LSAs throughout these chapters, inviting my imagined reader into a shared dialogic space through a series of reflective questions that I hope may have prompted them to bring their own ideas, insights and experiences into the frame. The readers of this text will ultimately have strong insights into what will work for their students along their educational journeys, and I hope I have, if anything, provided some useful food for thought along the way.

This book has also, in many ways, looked to the future as I have considered some core issues and themes that may come to shape the work of LSAs moving forward. My aim here has been to create a space for wider rumination and, indeed, further dialogue, inviting readers to reflect on their views and the architecture of future solutions. My other core goal with this work has been to examine the work of LSAs in a holistic frame, dispelling notions of the LSA as a note-taker and instead centring the intrinsically pastoral and pedagogical aspects of their work, much of which can go unacknowledged in education. There will, undoubtedly, be stones that I have left unturned and themes that are yet to be examined, and I hope that future LSAs may take inspiration from this work as they make their own contributions to the literature: always remember that your experience and knowledge matters as an LSA, and that there is a space for your voice within the inclusive educational discourse.

As this work draws to a close, I think it is important to focus on students, whose educational experience is integral to the work of LSAs. You will work with many different students over the course of your time as an LSA, each one of whom will be able to teach you something if you are open to learning it. The essence of your work rests on the supportive relationships that you build with them, and their safety, happiness, independence and positive educational progression are the cornerstones of your work together: listen to your students, laugh with them, make sure that your input adds value to what they are doing and craft an intentional space for their views to shape the course of your work together.

I will leave you with some final reflections and reminders…

Centre your work around the wellbeing of your students: your job is to make sure they feel happy and safe – future learning will flow from this.

Listen to your students and always lead with empathy: make conscious efforts to actively lean into their worldview and their frames of reference. It's important that you put aside your own assumptions and (potentially neurotypical) views about the world in order to do this.

Keep in mind that you will be, in many ways, seen as an academic role model both in the classroom and for your students more generally – bear this responsibility in mind, and be sure to model positive and pro-social behaviours.

Embrace the small wins: find the joy in the little things each day. Laughter helps a lot, and often this will help to build connection.

Look after your own wellbeing when working as an LSA: the risk of burnout is real, and you cannot pour from an empty cup. Take enough time to rest and reach out for support if you are struggling.

Relationships are the lifeblood of your work as an LSA: take the time to get to know your teaching colleagues and establish some trust and some good will. Remember that teachers have a lot on their plates: do what you can to help, and support your students together as a team – 'it should be very close collaborative work'.

Always contextualise challenging behaviour when it arises: remain calm in the face of it and remember that your job is to support your students in regulating their emotions and actions. 'Step down' heightened situations in the moment and focus on repairing relationships afterwards.

Dialogue is an end product in and of itself: it's always worth making time for dialogue with your students. Listen as they voice their views about the world and gently question them to help them refine their ideas.

Avoid task completion at all costs: your job is to foster independence and to help your students become as self-reliant as possible as they take the next step in their lives. Student independence is like an elastic band: 'Keep stretching the elastic all the time. How much independence can you give them? You're still there, but keep stretching it.'

Use technologies safely and wisely, to add value to your craft and to save time when you are in a pinch. Don't over-rely on them to do the pedagogical work for you: these skills may be time-consuming, but they are essential to the work of LSAs.

Ask for training as and when you need it: be empowered to ask for the things that you need to flourish as an LSA and don't hesitate to reach out to colleagues for information and support. Questions, as a rule of thumb, are good – lean on the expertise of fellow professionals, especially in the early days as you are finding your feet.

And finally, in the words of an LSA… 'Never forget the importance of the work you do – even if others sometimes undervalue it.'

Final reflective questions...

What are your personal takeaways from this book? Do you feel it has helped your SEND practice?

Has this book prompted you to view the work of LSAs from a different perspective? If so, how?

If you were to apply one insight or 'top tip' from this book to your own work, which one would it be and why?

Did any particular chapters or themes resonate with you or pique your interest over the course of your reading? If so, what were they and why?

Did you feel that this book has any conceptual blind spots? If so, what are they? Is there anything you felt that should have been included or expanded upon?

Has this work inspired you to make any future changes to your work as an LSA? If so, what are they and how might you weave them into your current routine?

Index

Note: page numbers in *italics* refer to Figures.

Aas, H. K. 31, 83
Abbott, L. 1
access to key learning materials 71, 75
active listening 42–44, 143, 146
Adams, R. 174
adaptive teaching 73
advocacy 24
agreements: student learner 102; teacher–TA 60
anxiety 20, 36, 52, 161, 170
apologies 104
approachability 96
art 113, 115, 166–167; and craft activities 48
artificial intelligence (AI) 152–153, 170–171; art 166–167; Copilot 152, 162–166; empathy gaps 153
assertiveness, gentle 47
assistive technologies for LSAs 7, 152–154, 169–172, 193; Copilot 152, 162–166; double screens 159–160; emails *see separate entry*; interdisciplinary learning support 168–169; iPads 155–157; reader pens 154–155; shared document editing 158–159; Teams *see separate entry*; virtual reality headsets 160–162; visual learning preferences 164–168
autonomy: LSA 186–187; student 49, 94, 132–134
AV1 robots 152

Barnes, D. 138
Basford, E. 60
Bauld, A. 35
Beltran, M. J. 48
Blatchford, P. 1, 140
body language 50, 67, 77

boundaries 88, 89; professional 39–42, 43, 55–56, 80
Bovill, C. 128
brainstorming 13, 65, 86, 88, 123, 156, 166
break duty 140
break times 41, 54–56, 67
breathing exercises 105
Breyer, C. 12, 27, 86, 174, 175
British Educational Research Association (BERA) 3–4

calmness 87–88, 105, 106
camaraderie 79–80, 116
career development 178
Cattan, S. 174
Cerbin, W. 31
chain of reasoning 164
challenges facing LSAs 20–23
challenging behaviour 5–6, 83, 106–107, 193; calm 87–88, 105, 106; contextualising student behaviour 84–86; de-escalation 87; mediative and restorative approaches 103–105; primary school students 105–106; rejection 90–94; role of LSA 83–84; student work reluctance 95–102; teachers, working with 88–90; triggers and stress points 86–87
Chang, Y. 52
character development 26
check-in method 93, 94, 111–115, 157
check-ins: student–LSA: small chats and 45–46, 87, 88; student–LSA: to discuss and review notes 118; teacher–LSA working relationship 74–75, 76, 89, 90–91
checklists, task 13, 91, 111, *112*, 122

195

Index

choice, student 49, 94, 95–96
chunking, task 12, 52, 105–106, 126–127, 162–164
Clarke, E. 12, 88–89
co-created learning 128–130, 138
cognitive empathy 31
communication, teacher–LSA 74–77; clear instructions 75–76; corridor chats 76; emails 64, 74, 76; float methods 91–93; visible 76
compassion 29, 31, 55, 85
connection(s) 28, 98; visual 167–168
consent: shadowing 180
consistency 69–70
continuing professional development (CPD) 177
Copilot 152, 162–166
Corbacho, A. M. 168
Cornell notes 117
corrections, in-class 67–68
Covid-19 pandemic 36
craft activities 48
Cremin, H. 2, 35; Sellman et al 104
cultural knowledge gaps 14–15

defining the LSA 4, 31–32, 193; at personal level 23–26; challenges 20–23; educational inclusion 11–15, 85–86; ethics of care 26–27; hidden aspects of role 18–20; individual factors shaping working practice 28–30; LSA/TA distinction 15–16; misconceptions 16–18; navigating neurotypical expectations 30–31; pedagogical component 13–15; relationship building 27–28
depression 35, 36, 170
dialogic ice-breakers 142
dialogic LSA 6–7, 29, 149–150; conversation vs dialogue 136–137; creating spaces for dialogue 141–144; meet student where they are 138–139; neurodivergent dialogic space 139–141; pivots 147–148; questioning 144–147; role of dialogue 137–139; younger age groups 148–149
dictation software, speech-to-text 155–157
doodle note-taking 167–168
double screens 159–160
drama 91, 113, 114
dual-working approaches 115–116
Dunlop-Bennett, E. 35

Education Health and Care Plan (EHCP) 21, 119
emails: completed assignments 104; detailed notes to students 93; LSA wellbeing 55, 56; support in class 93, 157–158; teacher–LSA working patterns 64, 74, 76
emojis/icons 165
emotional regulation 47, 71, 105
empathy 48; cognitive 31; gaps 153
enrichment activities 19, 48
epistemic humility 26, 137, 144, 147–148
epistemic injustice 16, 142
equity 24
essay: break down into key components 127; dictation software 156; digital editing software 158–159; plans 123
ethics 3–4, 153; of care 26–27
Ewert, A. 52
exam access arrangements 126, 154
exam past papers 126
exemplar answers 123–124
exercise and sport 53
expectations, setting realistic 101–102

Farrell, P. 2, 12
Fazackerley, A. 188
feedback 64, 158; digitally 159; and learning conversations 72–73; reciprocal 77–79, 115
Firth, J. 35
Fleming, N. 126
Fletcher, M. 152
float methods 91–93, 119–121, 187
formula sheets 71, 91, 122
Fox, G. 12
Fricker, M. 16, 142
Full-Time Equivalent (FTE) pay scales 185
fun 45, 56, 97, 146, 149, 166
future 7–8, 174–175, 188; day-to-day working improvements 186–188; pay reform 183–185; qualification 178–179; training, improvements to 175–177; understanding and appreciation 185–186

Garner, P. 2, 8
Garvie, D. 35
Geeson, R. 12
Genillard, T. 154
Gerschel, L. 6, 108

Index

Gidlund, U. 61
'give it a go' technique 124
goals 102; realistic 51, 52; written lesson 111
Google images 166–167
graphic novels 167
Gray, C. 1
grounded SEND knowledge 181–182
group-based approach 21
Guikas, I. 83, 88
Guilherme, A. 35
Guiney, D. 35
Gurney, P. W. 51

Hall, S. 2, 34
Hamilton, L. G. 30
help sheets and prompts 122
hierarchies, school 21–22
high-energy approach 50–51, 52
holistic view of education 26–27
homework 100–101
Hopwood, V. 6, 108
humour 45, 97
Husmann, P. 126, 164

inclusive education 11–15, 85–86
independence, student 6, 25, 56, 91, 108–109, 134, 193; autonomy, student 132–134; check-in method 111–115; co-created approach to learning 128–130; dual-working approaches 115–116; float methods 119–121; getting started 123–125; giving space 121, 131; holistic view of 109–111; in-class note-taking strategies 116–118; mistakes 130–131; one-to-one study sessions 123, 125–127; over-correction 130–131; ownership 131–132, 133; primary school students 127–128; reader pens 154–155; resource access 122, 124; seating 121; silences 130
information: ask if you are not sure 69; sensitive student 162; sharing key 63–64; sharing of lesson plans 72
inter-student teaching 129
interdisciplinary learning support 168–169
interests, student 97–99, 140–141, 143
internet 138; social media 50, 138
introductions 62–63, 71
Ion, M. 185
iPads 155–157

Joint Council for Qualifications (JCQ) 13

Kellert, S. 52
Kerslake, L. 137
Keyes, H. 48
kindness 27, 55
Kinman, G. 185
Kopp, B. 31
Kurian, N. 153

laughter 80, 193
learning conversations 133
learning games 143
learning theory: VARK (Visual, Auditory, Reading and Writing and Kinaesthetic) 126
Lee, A. 50
lessons: consistency 69–70; involvement in 64–66; over-contribution 65–66; positive and engaged outlook 66–67; sharing of lesson plans 72; student attendance 85–86; supportive presence 66–69
line managers 22, 44, 53, 54, 55, 106, 180
linear modes of thinking 169
listening, active 42–44, 143, 146
log of student support methods 54, 88
lunch duty 140
lunch times 41, 55–56, 67

McCluskey, G.: Sellman et al 104
McConkey, R. 1
McSorley, C. 36
Major, L. E. 174
Martin, L. 52
maths 69, 71, 116, 128, 169
mediative and restorative approaches 103–105
meditation 48
meetings, department 75
mental load of LSA work 22–23
mentoring 180–181
Microsoft: Copilot 152, 162–166; Teams *see separate entry*
mind maps 126, 165, 166, 167
mirroring 67, 87, 99–100
misconceptions 16–18
mistakes, leaving space for 130–131
mobile phones 56
model pro-social behaviours 19, 42, 85, 193
moment-to-moment pedagogy 19

Index

Morin, D. 83, 88
motivational strategies 50–52, 97
movement breaks 67, 72
Muijs, D. 1

nature and wellbeing 52–53
Navarro, M. F. 11, 18, 61
neurodiversity 17; concept of 30; dialogic space 139–141
neurotypical expectations 30–31
noise levels 68, 71–72
Norwich, B. 36
note-taking, in-class 15, 93, 116–118, 153
nudging 99

O'Brien, T. 2, 8, 35
obsessive compulsive disorder (OCD) 159
O'Loughlin, V. 126, 164
one-to-one study sessions 123, 125–127, 140, 146, 154, 157, 159, 169; shadowing 180
open-ended questions 3, 133, 145
openness 142
oracy 140–141, 142
othering 90
over-correction 130–131
over-reliance *see* independence, student
Owens, R. 117
ownership 131–132, 133

paired learning 129–130
Paju, B. 19
pastoral support 18–19; wellbeing support *see separate entry*
Pauk, W. 117
pay reform 183–185
pedagogy 13–15
Petty, S. 30
planning, preparation and assessment (PPA) time 179, 187
Point, Evidence, Explain, Link to Question (PEEL) paragraph structure 91, *92*, 120, 124
Pomodoro technique 96
positive reinforcement 51–52, 125, 126
post-work rituals 56
poverty 36
praise 51–52, 125
preferences, student 132–133
preparation time 179, 187

primary school students 12–13, 20, 34–35, 166; challenging behaviour 105–106; dialogic strategies 148–149; independence 127–128
Prince's Trust 36
problem solving 19
processing speeds 130
professional boundaries 39–42, 43, 55–56, 80
prompting 12, 126
prompts 158, 159, 163; Copilot 165; and helpsheets 122
pulse-check 122
punctuality 68

qualitative research 2–4; interview data 3
questions 144–147; 'call-out' 71; open-ended 3, 133, 145; reflective 145, 147–148

Raiyn, J. 164
rapport 28, 61, 69, 96, 103
reader pens 154–155
realistic expectations 101–102
reassurance 48–49, 162; solution-focused 85
record keeping 49, 73; log of student support methods 54, 88
reflective questions 145, 147–148
reinforcement, positive 51–52, 125, 126
rejection by student 90–94; taking step back 90–91
relationship building 27–28, 80, 143
reprimanding LSA 73
research support guides 13, *14*
resilience 18–20
resources, accessing materials and 21–22
rest breaks: LSAs 67, 106; students 46, 47–48, 52, 87, 89, 95, 96, 105–106, 165
restorative and mediative approaches 103–105
Reynolds, D. 1
Rodger, S. H. 164
routines 100–101

safeguarding 36–37, 55, 56
Savage, M. 185
scaffolding 175–176; roadmaps 91, 162–164

scribing 12, 126, 153
seating 121
second pair of eyes 68
self-concept 18, 51
self-esteem 18, 50, 51, 52
Sellman, E. 5, 104
sensory sensitivities 86
sentence starters 13, 124
service to others 24
shadowing 179–180
Shor, I. 128
signposting 38–39
silences 130, 142; silent working in class 71–72
Sirkko, R. 19
Skipp, A. 6, 108
social embarrassment 90, 91, 93, 113
social engagement 19–20, 26, 128
social media 50, 138
social prompt strategy 20
social scripts 136
social skills 19
socialisation 18, 19, 42, 138
soft skills 80
special interests 97–99, 140–141, 143
speech-to-text dictation software 155–157
split screen 160
sport 53
step back, taking 88, 90–91, 187; *see also* independence, student
storyboards 166
study methods 126
study skills 13
study spaces 100–101
subject confidence 22

task: attempt 15 minutes of 96, 102, 126; boards 128; checklists 13, 91, 111, *112*, 122; chunking 13, 52, 105–106, 126–127, 162–164; purpose 98–99; skeleton outline of 123–124
teacher–LSA working patterns 5, 21–22, 81; actively supporting teachers 79, 89; camaraderie 79–80; challenging behaviour 88–90; communication strategies 74–77; consistency 69–70; contextual specificity 60–61; dialogue 142; float methods 91–93, 120, 187; helping hand 68–69; mutual trust and teamwork 77–79, 89; top tips for LSAs 62–70; top tips for teachers 70–74

teaching assistants 15–16
Teams 86, 93, 113, 157, 158; LSA wellbeing 56; teacher–LSA working patterns 71, 76
teamwork 75, 78–79, 89; skills audit of team 180
think-aloud method 148–149
time management 100; 20 minutes to engage 88; attempt 15 minutes of task 96, 102, 126
timers 125–126
timetables, visual 164–166
Trafford, A. 36
training 44, 54, 60, 171, 174–175, 193; access to 176–177; access to qualification 178–179; balance of in-person and online 176; bridging gap between theory and practice 181–183; challenge higher-ability students 176; dedicated time for 177, 179, 187; future improvements to 175–177; knowledge gaps 178; mentoring 180–181; scaffolding 175–176; shadowing 179–180
transcripts, lesson 157
travel skills 111, 161–162
triad working structure 73
triage work tasks 55
triggers and stress points 86–87
trust and respect, mutual 77–79
Twenge, J. 36

Van Heijst, B. F. 35
VARK (Visual, Auditory, Reading and Writing and Kinaesthetic) learning theory 126
velcro LSA 108–109, 121, 134
virtual reality headsets 160–162
Visser, J. 88–89
visual learning preferences 164–168
visual timetables 164–166

Wagner, C. 138, 141, 142
Wang, J. 164
Watson, D. 21
Webster, R. 1, 2, 34
Wegerif, R. 2, 29, 136–137, 138, 144, 147, 149
wellbeing support 4–5, 57; active listening 42–44; art and craft activities 48; central role of 34–36; definition of wellbeing 35; gentle assertiveness

199

47; for LSAs 53–56, 88, 106; meditation 48; motivational strategies 50–52; nature and wellbeing 52–53; professional boundaries 39–42, 43, 55–56; reassurance 48–49; record keeping 49; rest breaks 46, 47–48, 52; safeguarding 36–37, 55, 56; signposting 38–39; small chats and check-ins 45–46; student choice 49

Weston, A. 152, 162, 170
Wharmby, P. 140, 141
Wilson, E. 52
Wittgenstein, L. 136
word(s): banks 122; clarity around key 149
working space 42–43
workload 21
Wright, N. 36

For Product Safety Concerns and Information please contact our EU
representative GPSR@taylorandfrancis.com
Taylor & Francis Verlag GmbH, Kaufingerstraße 24, 80331 München, Germany

www.ingramcontent.com/pod-product-compliance
Lightning Source LLC
Chambersburg PA
CBHW070316240426
43661CB00057B/2660